# Resources for Teaching History: 14–16

## Also available from Continuum

*Resources for Teaching History: 11–14*, Susie Hodge
*The History Teacher's Handbook*, Neil Smith
*100+ Ideas for Teaching History*, Julia Murphy

# Resources for Teaching History: 14–16

Susie Hodge

continuum

A companion website to accompany this book is available online at:
http://education.hodge2.continuumbooks.com
Please visit the link and register with us to receive your password and to access these downloadable resources.
If you experience any problems accessing the resources, please contact Continuum at:
info@continuumbooks.com

**Continuum International Publishing Group**
The Tower Building
11 York Road
London
SE1 7NX

80 Maiden Lane, Suite 704
New York, NY 10038

www.continuumbooks.com



As this book was going to press a new coalition government was making changes within education, so references to the TDA, QCDA and any other governmental website may no longer be completely up-to-date.

**British Library Cataloguing-in-Publication Data**
A catalogue record for this book is available from the British Library.

ISBN: 9780826422385 (paperback)

**Library of Congress Cataloging-in-Publication Data**
Hodge, Susie, 1960-
Resources for teaching history: 14–16 / Susie Hodge
p. cm. — (Resources for teaching)
ISBN 978-0-8264-2238-5 (pbk.)
1. History—Study and teaching (Secondary)—Great Britain. I. Title.
II. Series

D16.4.G7H633 2010
907.1'241—dc22 2009047752

Typeset by Pindar NZ, Auckland, New Zealand
Printed and bound in Great Britain by Bell & Bain Ltd, Glasgow

Mixed Sources
Product group from well-managed forests and other controlled sources
www.fsc.org Cert no. TT-COC-002769
© 1996 Forest Stewardship Council
FSC

# Contents

## Section E: Germany



## Section F: America



## Section G: International relations (2)



## Section H: World War II

## Section I: The Cold War

# Introduction

Designed to assist busy teachers of History for the 14–16 age range, this book is a user-friendly bank of lessons, informed by exam board specifications and current ideas about teaching and learning. Whether you are teaching a full or short course in GCSE Modern World History, the skills and knowledge that students are required to attain remains similar and all lessons are aimed to support your teaching, including a wide range of ideas and activities for individual, pair and group work. There are suggestions for various methods of delivering lessons, all aimed to encourage students' understanding of the subject and their engagement with the past.

### Reinforcing learning

By strengthening students' understanding of the causes, effects and consequences of relevant historical events and encouraging them to research, select, analyse and explain their findings, the lessons in this book will help you to facilitate your students' historical skills. Lessons are designed to help students interpret, comprehend and evaluate appropriate aspects of history, using a range of resources and sources. The lessons give students opportunities to make reasoned judgements and to use informed and substantiated knowledge in various ways, often investigating themes from political, economical, technological, scientific, social, religious, cultural and aesthetic perspectives.

Few students will come from Key Stage 3 completely prepared to apply these skills, so in many of the lessons, activities will assist the development of their understanding and analytical skills, helping to provoke challenging enquiries and thorough investigations. Students will engage in tasks that help them to process information, so increasing their understanding of historical contexts and improving their communication skills.

### Augmenting your teaching

These lessons do not cover an entire GCSE course, but are here to augment and reinforce your teaching. Unless otherwise stated, most lessons are planned to take about one hour but you can easily adapt them to suit your classes and your timetable, for example, by skipping the starter or using the tips for differentiation. Generally lessons are organized chronologically. Some begin in the middle or at the end of a topic, and some suggest opportunities to expand on topics that you might have already covered. In some places, there is some overlap between what your students will have learned in earlier years and the areas they are investigating for GCSE. Covering a topic again can help to boost students' confidence and strengthen their understanding at a more mature and comprehensive level.

### Assessment objectives

Assessment objectives are comparable across the various exam board specifications. All encourage learners to be inspired by following a coherent and worthwhile course of study, so assessment objectives are covered in all lessons. Here are general explanations of the three assessment objectives for History at this level (from: http://www.ofqual.gov.uk/files/qca-07–3454_gcsecriteriahistory.pdf):

- Recall, select and communicate their knowledge and understanding of history
- Demonstrate their understanding of the past through explanation and analysis of:
  - key concepts: causation, consequence, continuity, change and significance within a historical context
  - key features and characteristics of the periods studied and the relationships between them
- Understand, analyse and evaluate:
  - a range of source material as part of a historical enquiry
  - how aspects of the past have been interpreted and represented in different ways as part of a historical enquiry

- All GCSE History specifications require students to demonstrate knowledge and understanding through:
  - making connections and comparisons between different aspects of the periods, themes and topics studied
  - describing, analysing and evaluating the causes and consequences of historical events and situations
  - describing, analysing and evaluating changes and developments in the periods, themes and topics studied
  - assessing the significance of individuals, events, developments and/or ideas in the history studied.

### Building on Key Stage 3

Students' experiences at Key Stage 3 can vary considerably even in the same school, depending on various factors such as different teachers, availability of materials and lessons during their initial years at secondary school. While the National Curriculum at Key Stages 2 and 3 covers certain aspects of history, there can be great variety in individual interpretation and teaching, so it is always helpful to start the beginning of a topic by finding out what your students already know, so you can build on their understanding of significant ideas and concepts.

### Exam board requirements

All the major exam boards – that is, OCR, AQA and EDEXCEL as well as SQA and WJEC – require students to acquire knowledge and understanding of certain aspects of history, learning how the past has been represented and interpreted. All lessons here are designed to help develop your students' historical understanding and to help them learn to organize and communicate their knowledge of key concepts, to draw conclusions and to appreciate that these are liable to reassessment in the light of new or reinterpreted evidence.

### How this book is organized

The book contains nearly eighty lessons that can be adapted to suit your needs and the needs of your students. All are aimed to help them become more accustomed to the types of learning they need for success at GCSE. Although this is a flexible resource, if you begin a topic (for example, World War I) it works best to complete that series of lessons with the class. Icons at the top of the Teacher's Sheet indicate where a lesson would be best delivered, with the students having access to the internet or books for research. All lessons encourage active participation and suggest a number of ways of approaching subjects, in order to develop appropriate skills. They are designed to help your students to get better results, but they also need to prepare for their exam wisely. At the end of each topic or term, it's a good idea to give your students a test to help them prepare for GCSE. Also, once they have completed each subject, encourage them to write out a list of topics to revise. At the end of the course, they should produce their own revision timetables and take ownership of their own revision plans. The most successful students revise regularly and on a wide variety of topics. A useful website is:

http://www.schoolhistory.co.uk/revision/

A variety of methods and approaches are covered in each lesson in this book, giving breadth to the skills and knowledge your students will attain. Each lesson gives timings for every element, including explaining their homework. Each homework should take students between 30 and 45 minutes to complete. Within this book, every lesson includes the following:

1. Introduction
2. Aims and outcomes
3. Starter
4. Main phase
5. Plenary
6. Suggestion for homework

7. Make it easier!
8. Make it harder!

**Key to icons**

There are two icons, which appear throughout the text.

ICT equipment or computers required for this lesson

Extra print resources (text books, dictionaries, etc.) required for this lesson

Having these resources available will enhance the learning, but in most cases the teacher can easily adapt the plan to conduct the lesson without ICT or textbooks, if necessary.

# Section A Reforms in Britain in the 20th century

# 1 Poverty reforms in Britain

**Introduction:** This lesson will introduce students to the situation in Britain before the poverty reforms of the early twentieth century. It will help them to understand why reforms were necessary at the time and why attitudes to the poor changed.

**Aims and outcomes:** At the end of the lesson, all students will be aware of the conditions of the poor at the end of the nineteenth century and beginning of the twentieth century, and of the lack of assistance given to them by more affluent members of society. Most students will be aware of the need for change in society and why this was particularly important at the time. Some students will understand the implications of the government taking responsibility for the poor for the first time.

**Starter (20–25 minutes):** Introduce some facts about poverty at the turn of the century in Britain. Explain that poor people did not live in the same sorts of conditions that poor people do today. For instance, many did not have possessions such as shoes, washing machines, guaranteed food to eat or access to any money from the government. Show the class some images of or information on early twentieth century poverty (some links to useful examples are provided online).

In small groups of up to four, students are to study the images and within their groups see what they can deduce about them. They should discuss: What do the images tell us about poverty at the turn of the twentieth century? After about 10 minutes, each group should select one or two spokespeople to stand up and present to the rest of the class what they have gathered about the lives of poor people before government reforms.

**Main phase (25 minutes):** Display the background information sheet provided online and read the information to the class. Then ask the students to answer the questions on their task sheets, using a range of resources.

**Plenary (5–10 minutes):** Together with the whole class, create a mind map about why social reforms were needed. Draw it on the board, as students draw it in their exercise books or on paper or, if you have the software, on a computer, and ask students to suggest how it develops.

**Suggestion for homework (5 minutes):** For the next lesson, students are to find out what the Liberal government did to help the poor. They should find out details of two of the reforms, choosing from the following:

1. The *Education Act 1906* – local councils were given the power to provide school meals to children from the poorest families.
2. The *Education Act 1907* – compulsory and free medical checks for all students.
3. The *Children's Act 1908* – parents could be prosecuted for cruelty against their children. Also, specially built Borstals were built for young offenders.
4. The *Pensions Act 1908* – weekly pensions were given to the elderly if they had worked to the best of their abilities during their working lives.
5. The *Labour Exchanges Act 1909* set up labour exchanges where unemployed workers could go to look for a job.
6. The *National Insurance Act (Part II) 1911* – insurance scheme where workers had to pay a certain amount to insure themselves against sickness. If they fell ill and couldn't work, they were given sick pay.
7. The *National Insurance Act (Part II) 1911* insured workers against any unemployed periods.

(*continued over page 4*)

# Poverty reforms in Britain

**Your task**

Use a range of different resources to research the following:

1. What caused the change in attitude towards the poor?
2. What was New Liberalism?
3. Who was Charles Booth and what did he do?
4. Who was Seebohm Rowntree and what did he do?
5. Why did the Boer War have an effect on the people and government's opinions about the poor?
6. Why did the two leading Liberal politicians, David Lloyd George and Winston Churchill, believe in social reform?
7. What was the new political party, when did it form and in what ways did it affect the decisions of the Liberal Party?
8. What is meant by: a) the poverty line and b) the welfare state?

**Useful resources**

http://www.learningcurve.gov.uk/britain1906to1918/g1/background.htm
http://www.bbc.co.uk/schools/gcsebitesize/history/mwh/britain/liberalreformsrev1.shtml
http://www.bbc.co.uk/scotland/learning/bitesize/higher/history/liberal/
http://www.nationalarchives.gov.uk/education/britain1906to1918/g1/gallery1.htm

**Make it easier!**

Some students will find it difficult to uncover the depth of information necessary. Show by example, perhaps using a more able student, how considered their answers should be. If possible, provide a range of resources designed for different abilities; some books, for example, are written for Foundation or Higher Levels.

**Make it harder!**

For lessons early on in the GCSE course in particular, make sure that students more able to research and write do not lower their expectations, which can happen while you are busily trying to help the less able. Emphasize that they should always try to investigate deeper rather than broader (about less but in-depth rather than about more but skimming the surface). If possible, show them previous exemplary work or do your own example to show them your expectations.

# TIPS: for mind mapping

Explain to students that 'social reform' is your starting point. From those two words, you can expand in any direction. They can mention any words or topics that they think are relevant (and will have to explain why). Draw branches leading off the central heading and encourage your students to think broadly, expanding on the ideas that emerge. Don't think about ideas in too much detail, but put them all down. If you're doing this on a whiteboard or interactive whiteboard, then you can also ask members of the class to suggest where to put topics and if they need moving and so on. If you can't think of where a certain word or topic should go, then jot it down in a list to the side of the mind map and see if you can fit it in at the end. Use colour to clarify things if necessary – be as creative as you and your students like. (They will remember more through colour). Some free mind mapping downloadable material is available on the internet, or your school might buy a special programme, but creating one as a class is often far more rewarding and encourages creative thinking.

Quick quiz: If you have students in the class who finish early, give them the following to look up on the internet and find out meanings for:

- Laissez-faire
- Self-help
- The Majority Report
- The Minority Report
- Three basic differences of policies of the Conservatives, the Liberals and the Labour Party in 1906.

Give awards, such as house points or leaving the class first, for those who find out all the correct answers the quickest.

# 2 Opposition to poverty reforms

**Introduction:** This lesson gives students the opportunity to consider the reforms introduced by Lloyd George and Churchill, and how and why many opposed them.

**Aims and outcomes:** At the end of the lesson, all students will know how many wealthier people felt about the new government's reforms. Most students will understand reasons that the government took certain approaches initially and the difficulties and consequences of the early reforms and some students will realize the problems faced by Lloyd George, Churchill and the rest of the Liberal government.

**Starter (10–15 minutes):** Discuss the findings of the last lesson and why some social groups were more at risk of falling into poverty than others. Explain how the Reform Acts of 1867 and 1884 had given the vote to working-class men and the Liberal Party realized that working-class men would welcome reforms for the poor, which was one of the reasons they introduced them. Next, discuss the last homework, that is, what were the reforms of the new 'welfare state' created by the Liberal government after 1906? Make sure that everyone makes notes and that many join in with the discussions.

**Main phase (40 minutes):** How did David Lloyd George, as Chancellor of the Exchequer, pay for the reforms of 1906–11? Talk about the budget of 1909, which taxed the rich and landowners. Why do students think the House of Lords opposed the budget of 1909? Using a range of resources, students are to research and make notes on the questions on their task sheets (these are also available online for you to display on the whiteboard). The first eight questions should be done individually, before pairing up for the remaining 16 questions.

**Plenary (5 minutes):** There is a lot to pack in during this lesson! If you have time, students should share some of their findings with the rest of the class. Ask who found uncovering some facts difficult, and if so, which, and does anyone have any tips or information?

**Suggestion for homework (5 minutes):** Everyone should make sure that they are clear on all points discussed and researched over the last two lessons. Notes should be completed and any questions noted for the next lesson. Everyone should make sure that they have notes on everything covered in the lessons, plus:

1. The effectiveness of the government's reforms.
2. Why the government introduced reforms in the first place and who they helped.
3. By 1914, how far the welfare state was established.
4. Through events, how the government changed between 1906 and 1919.

**Make it easier!**
Some less able students might lack confidence, so give as much individual guidance as you can with some suggestions about how and where to research and how to articulate their answers. Explain what aspects are important to look out for as some may find it difficult to select and use information.

**Make it harder!**
Make sure that more able students give detailed answers that have been thoroughly researched and written in full sentences.

# Opposition to poverty reforms

## Part 1

How did David Lloyd George, as Chancellor of the Exchequer, pay for the reforms of 1906–11? Using a range of resources, research and make notes on the following:

1. What was self-help?
2. Who was Charles Booth and where did he carry out research about the poor?
3. What did Seebohm Rowntree discover?
4. Why and how were the Liberal reforms criticized by some?
5. Why did these critics think that the state shouldn't help?
6. How were the Liberal reforms paid for?
7. Who received old-age pensions and were they adequate?
8. Health insurance and unemployment insurance – who did and who didn't receive these?

## Part 2

With a partner, answer the following:

1. How did the *1906 Education Act* help children?
2. What was a weakness of the *1906 Education Act*?
3. How did children benefit from the *1907 Education Act*?
4. What was a weakness of the *1907 Education Act*?
5. How did the *Children and Young Persons Act of 1908* protect children?
6. What happened to young offenders after that?
7. Who benefited from the *Pension Act of 1908*?
8. Give two ways in which pensions did not solve the problem for poor old people.
9. What was the purpose of Labour Exchanges?
10. Give one reason why Labour Exchanges were successful.
11. Give one weakness of Labour Exchanges.
12. What problem did the *National Insurance Act (Part I)* deal with?
13. How was it paid for and how did people benefit from it?
14. Why did workers resent the *1911 National Insurance Act (Part II)?*
15. How much benefit did unemployed workers get through this scheme?
16. Why did unemployment pay not solve the problem for poor people? Give two reasons.

# 3 Welfare and reform

**Introduction:** This lesson helps students to consider the budget and the welfare reforms of the Liberal government of 1906–14.

**Aims and outcomes:** At the end of the lesson, all students will be aware of the Liberal reforms of 1906–14. Most students will understand the connotations of the budget and taxing that the government put into place in 1909 and some students will recognize the reasons for the conflicts in society and other reasons for the changes that occurred during the early twentieth century.

**Starter (10 minutes):** Students should work in small groups or pairs to discuss and research for 5–10 minutes and then produce individual charts on 'dealing with the causes of poverty'. The charts should consist of five columns under the headings: Childhood; Old age; Sickness; Unemployment and Low wages. Under these headings, they should describe the relevant reforms, when they were started and their strengths and weaknesses.

**Main phase (35–40 minutes):** Encourage everyone to join in with a discussion about why the Liberal government brought in welfare reforms. Write some of the points on the board and ask students to make a mind map to elucidate. Next, explain to the class how David Lloyd George, as Chancellor of the Exchequer, was responsible for finding the money to pay for the reforms and how he did this in the controversial budget of 1909 by raising taxes. Discuss who would have opposed this and why it became known as the People's Budget. You could display and read through the information provided online at this point.

There are some useful web resources online for students of a variety of abilities, to give them some information on the topic.

Students are to write an essay, explaining all they have learned about the Liberal reforms, the budget, the opposition and the situation in Britain at the time. In the essay, they should explain what measures the government introduced and how these helped people – or not. They should include who opposed the reforms and why. Finally students must draw their own conclusions as to whether or not they believe that the Liberal government of 1906–14 started the welfare state. They should use their mind maps, charts and any other resources available to them to plan the essay and help them to thoughtful and relevant conclusions.

**Plenary (10 minutes):** Show everyone a contemporary poster, such as:

http://www.learningcurve.gov.uk/britain1906to1918/g2/cs4/images/g2cs4s1.jpg
http://www.nationalarchives.gov.uk/education/britain1906to1918/g2/cs4/g2cs4s1.htm

Ask why this poster was a form of propaganda. Try to extract valid reasons about the wording and images, what propaganda is and why this poster demonstrates that.

Ask the class to explain what the image is 'saying'.

**Suggestions for homework (5 minutes):** All students should complete their essays, making sure that they are thorough and coherent.

**Make it easier!**

Less able students may need some sentence starters or further guidance about planning their essays.

**Make it harder!**

More able students should be encouraged to be as thorough as possible. Give them a list of points to include in their essays.

# Welfare and reform

## Part 1

In your work book, along with the class discussion, make a quick mind map about why the Liberal government brought in welfare reforms.

## Part 2

David Lloyd George was Chancellor of the Exchequer and so responsible for finding the money to pay for the reforms. He did this in the controversial budget of 1909 by raising taxes. Who do you think would have opposed this? Why did it become known as the People's Budget?

Here is a useful web resource:

http://www.bbc.co.uk/schools/gcsebitesize/history/mwh/britain/liberalreformsrev3.shtml

Ultimately, the Liberal reforms were not enormously effective as they were quite moderate and there was little redistribution from the rich to the poor. The *National Insurance Acts*, for instance, meant that those workers who received benefits had paid for them anyway. So, although this Liberal government went further than any previous government in using State resources to help aspects of society, many historians argue that it was not enough to create a welfare state.

## Part 3

Plan and write an essay, explaining all you have learned about the Liberal reforms, the budget, the opposition and the situation in Britain at the time.

- Explain what measures the government introduced and how these helped people – or not.
- Include who opposed the reforms and why?
- Draw your own conclusions – do you believe that the Liberal government of 1906–14 started the welfare state?

For an effective essay, use your mind map, charts and any other resources available to plan the essay and help you to reach thoughtful and relevant conclusions. Plan your essay in your work book.

# 4 Votes for women (1)

**Introduction:** This lesson continues from any introduction students may have had to the subject in Key Stage 3.

**Aims and outcomes:** At the end of the lesson, all students will understand that not everyone had the vote at the turn of the twentieth century and why many considered this wrong. All students will be aware of the position of women in society in 1900. Most students will understand many of the differences between the Suffragists and the Suffragettes; their aims, methods, leaders and effectiveness; and some students will understand why women's rights were emerging as a major issue at this point in history and what arguments were used for and against allowing women to have the vote.

**Starter (10 minutes):** Introduce the position of women in society in 1900. There are some facts and background information in the online resources that you could display on the whiteboard.

Working in small groups of two to four, students should produce a table showing arguments for and against women getting the vote at the turn of the twentieth century.

**Main phase (40 minutes):** Display and/or read aloud the background information. Then, remaining in their groups, students are to research the Suffragists and the Suffragettes. They are to create a second table in their books – individually, although they can research and discuss within their groups. The tables should be divided into two columns and include:

1. The main protagonists of each movement
2. What each group – the NUWSS and WSPU – stood for
3. The aims and approaches of the two groups

Next, remaining in their groups, students should discuss and list at least three reasons why women began wanting the vote at this point in time. A list of possible reasons is available online that you might like to display to the class or print off before the lesson.

**Plenary (10 minutes):** Select four gregarious students to take on the roles of Millicent Fawcett, Emmeline Pankhurst, Christabel Pankhurst and Sylvia Pankhurst. Give them the following descriptions and ask them to introduce themselves to the class (you can also find these character descriptions online). The rest of the class should ask the four characters questions about their beliefs and activities. You could start by giving some of the 'audience' questions, asking them to pretend that they are journalists interviewing these historical figures, such as: (to Millicent) why did you choose a peaceful approach? This question and more for the other characters are available online. You may need to help the 'actors' with their answers.

*Millicent Fawcett*
My older sister, Elizabeth Garrett, tried to qualify as a doctor but as a woman, came across opposition. In 1865, my other sister Louise took me to hear a speech on women's rights by the MP, John Stuart Mill. It was wonderful. In 1857, I married Henry Fawcett, an MP, who had been blinded in a shooting accident. He was a great supporter of women's rights and through his encouragement; I joined the London Suffrage Committee in 1868. By the early 1880s, I had become one of the leaders. Henry died in 1884 and in 1890; I was elected president of the National Union of Women's Suffrage Societies (NUWSS). I remained committed to the use of legitimate methods to gain votes for women although I admired the Suffragette's courage.

(*continued over page 12*)

# Votes for women (1)

Within your group, research the Suffragists and the Suffragettes. Once you have discussed your findings sensibly, create a second table in your book. Divide the table into two columns and include:

1. The main protagonists of each movement
2. What each group – the NUWSS and WSPU – stood for
3. The aims and approaches of the two groups

Finally, discuss with your group and list at least three reasons why women began wanting the vote at this point in time.

*Emmeline Pankhurst*

I was born in 1858. My mother was a passionate feminist and took me to women's suffrage meetings in the early 1870s. At 21, I married a lawyer, Richard, who was also a strong supporter of women's suffrage. We had five children. In 1895, I became a Poor Law Guardian, which involved regular visits to the local workhouse. I was horrified by the suffering of the people there, particularly the way women were treated, which reinforced my belief that women's suffrage was the only way to solve these problems. In 1903, I founded the Women's Social and Political Union (WSPU), limiting membership exclusively to women. Our motto was 'Deeds not Words'.

*Christabel Pankhurst*

As Emmeline's eldest daughter, I was one of the few women to train as a lawyer in the 1890s, but as a woman, I was not allowed to work as a lawyer. I became involved with the NUWSS in 1901 with my mother and sister Sylvia. By 1903, however, we became frustrated by the Suffragists' lack of success and we formed the Women's Social and Political Union (WSPU). We believed that to make others notice us, Suffragettes should be more militant. In 1905, I disrupted a Liberal Party meeting with a friend. We were arrested and after we were imprisoned, many more women joined the WSPU.

*Sylvia Pankhurst*

Born in 1882, I trained as an artist. Like my parents and sister, I became a member of the new Labour Party and began working for the Women's Social and Political Union (WSPU), founded by my mother in 1903. She disapproved of me spending so much time with poor working women and not focusing on the right to vote. In 1906 I left the Royal College of Art and worked full-time for the WSPU. In 1911 my book *The History of the Women's Suffrage Movement* was published. When WSPU women began setting fire to buildings, I left and concentrated on helping the Labour Party build up its support in London.

**Suggestion for homework (5 minutes):** Each student should write a short passage, explaining why women wanted the vote, particularly at this time and comparing the differences between the Suffragists and the Suffragettes.

**Make it easier!**

Less able students could work in pairs or groups of three to produce the tables between them.

**Make it harder!**

More able students could work in a small group and produce two posters explaining the case for the women's suffrage and the case against the women's suffrage.

# TIPS: Votes for Women Topic Tips

- Make sure that all your students recognize the differences between the Suffragists and the Suffragettes.
- Make sure that they understand why so many were against their aims (e.g. women might neglect their homes and families if they became interested in politics; women's brains were not formed the same as men's, they were irrational and so would make absurd choices; women were too emotional; the Liberals thought they would all vote for Conservatives and the Conservatives thought they would all vote for Liberals; many women thought it was too masculine a subject for women to be involved with).
- All students should be aware of why the Suffragettes became so extreme after 1912.
- All students should be clear about 'proper' names and essential dates, such as the formation of the National Union of the Women's Suffrage Societies (1897) and the Women's Social and Political Union (1903).
- In 1800, few 'ordinary' people could vote, but by 1850, some women began to complain about this. By 1900, most working men could vote in general elections. All your students need to be clear about the reasons why many believed that women *should* be able to vote, and why many believed that they should not. Remind them of British society's respect for the monarch – and what Queen Victoria believed about women getting the vote.

# 5 Votes for women (2)

**Introduction:** This lesson introduces students to the activities of the Suffragettes and the corresponding reaction of the government.

**Aims and outcomes:** At the end of the lesson, all students should know about some of the tactics used by the Suffragettes to gain publicity for their cause. Most students will recognize the desperation and frustration that triggered their actions and the attitude of the government towards them. Some students will be aware of the opposition between the government and the Suffragettes and some will be able to draw relevant conclusions about the effectiveness of the Suffragettes methods.

**Starter (10–15 minutes):** Give the class a bit of background about women's rights and the formation of the Suffragettes (there is an information sheet online). Explain to students that Emmeline Pankhurst (1858–1928) was the leader of the Women's Social and Political Union that formed in 1903. After a meeting in 1906 with Herbert Asquith, Britain's Liberal prime minister, she lost hope of winning the vote and began resorting to militant tactics. They should read the excerpt of a speech made by Mrs Pankhurst in March 1908. This is available online for you to project onto the whiteboard or to print out and give to the students to read. Invite a class discussion about the speech. Do students believe that Emmeline Pankhurst's speech was convincing? If so, what was strong about it? If not, what should she have said to rouse support?

**Main phase (35–40 minutes):** What were the arguments for and against the women's suffrage and how effective were the activities of the Suffragettes? Everyone is to write a short essay on the topic, researching with available resources.

Talk to the class about publicity and propaganda. Does everyone understand why the Suffragettes took a more militant approach than the Suffragists? Do they think that this was the right approach? Would a different approach have been more successful? Did some of their methods set the cause back or did it propel the cause into public consciousness? Explain some of the things the Suffragettes did to draw attention to their cause. There is a list of facts online that you might like to use at this point.

**Plenary (5–10 minutes):** After students have planned and started writing their essays, take some minutes to ask around the class, reviewing what has been learned so far and what progress has been made on the essays.

**Suggestion for homework (5 minutes):** Students should finish their essays started in class.

**Make it easier!**

Some students might have only managed to plan their essays during the lesson while others may have made a good start. It is not always the most able that make the most progress during the lesson, so keep checking and discussing with individuals how they are proceeding. Explain to everyone that depth rather than breadth is important at this stage – they should all delve deeply to find relevant information.

**Make it harder!**

More able students could write a bulleted list of the similarities and differences between the two groups of protestors.

# Votes for women (2)

You are to write a short essay on the arguments for and against the women's suffrage and how effective were the activities of the Suffragettes, using any available resources.

# 6 Votes for women (3)

**Introduction:** This lesson will help students to recap on what they know about the women's suffrage.

**Aims and outcomes:** At the end of the lesson, all students should understand the beliefs about women that were held by most people in the nineteenth century and why the women's suffrage developed. All will be aware of the reasons why women did eventually get the vote. Most students will be aware of the inequalities that women faced during that period and the methods and consequences of their actions. Some students will recognize particular injustices faced by women at the time and will be aware of some repercussions of their actions.

**Starter (10 minutes):** Ask the class what is important about being allowed to vote? Why did women feel that they should be allowed to vote? Show them images and ask them to explain what each image is about and to give their opinions about them. A list of links for a variety of images including women being force-fed in prison can be found online, or you can use your own pictures.

**Main phase (35–40 minutes):** Explain to the students about the Cat and Mouse Act (there is an information sheet online should you like to use it), then using whatever other resources they can, ask students to research and answer the questions on their task sheets, writing in full sentences.

Next, recap on the actions of the Suffragettes and tell the class that they might have become even more violent, but in August 1914, Europe was thrust into World War I. Immediately they ceased their campaign and set about supporting their country. Many women worked in munitions factories or became drivers, engineers or worked on the land and some became nurses. The work that women did was crucial for Britain's war effort and in 1918; the *Representation of the People Act* was passed by Parliament. This allowed property-owning women over thirty the right to vote. Ten years later, all women were given the vote on equal terms with men.

**Plenary (10 minutes):** Students should exchange their answers and mark each other's work. Then discuss whether actions change things? What do students think about the actions of the Suffragettes and Suffragists? Were any or all of their actions justified?

**Suggestion for homework (5 minutes):** Each student should create a poster advertising the women's suffrage. It should be succinct, clear and eye-catching, telling everyone why it is important for women to have the vote.

**Make it easier!**
Less able students might need an even firmer structure for their research, but don't remove their independence, so try to gauge what they need.

**Make it harder!**
More able students should be reminded to include plenty of relevant details.

# Votes for women (3)

Using further resources, research and answer the following questions, writing in full sentences:

1. Give three reasons why women wanted the vote at the end of the nineteenth century.
2. What was Queen Victoria's opinion of the women's suffrage?
3. What were members of the NUWSS known as?
4. What were members of the WSPU known as?
5. Give the names of the three Pankhurst women involved in the founding of the WSPU.
6. What was Winston Churchill and Sir Edward Grey's reaction to Christabel and Annie Kenney's disruption of their meeting in 1905?
7. What happened to Emily Davison in June 1913?
8. What was the authorities' reaction to women on hunger strikes in prison?
9. What Act did they pass because of the hunger strikes?
10. What did the Suffragettes do to David Lloyd George's house?

# Section B World War I

# 7 Women and the First World War

**Introduction:** This lesson will introduce students to the efforts of women during World War I, showing how they contributed to the war effort.

**Aims and outcomes:** At the end of the lesson, all students will understand the efforts that women made during World War I. Most students will be able to make sound judgements as to whether or not their war efforts had more or less effect on the women's suffrage. Some students will understand the connotations of women entering the workforce, even though at the time it was because of the war – they will recognize how this changed the perception of women forever.

**Starter (10–15 minutes):** Explain to the class that historians disagree over whether the Suffragettes' methods damaged rather than furthered their cause. Ask the class what they believe and work out a chart on the board 'for' and 'against' the Suffragettes' methods. If possible, select some members of the class to create this. They must be sensible and stand by the board, taking suggestions from the rest of the class and writing relevant pros and cons of the Suffragettes in the chart.

**Main phase (35–40 minutes):** Direct students to read their task sheets. In pairs, they are to research the jobs that women did to contribute to the war effort. They should list the jobs, explaining what they were and what women did. There is a list for those students struggling to start online.

**Plenary (5–10 minutes):** Ask the class whether they think that Parliament gave women the vote in 1918 because of the efforts they made during the war or because of the tactics of the Suffragettes? Discuss this for 10 minutes in preparation for an essay for homework.

**Suggestion for homework (5 minutes):** Did the government allow women the vote in 1918 because of the tactics of the Suffragettes prior to the war or because of women's work during the war?



**Make it easier!**
The list of women's work during the war is one way you can help less able students in this lesson. You could also help some students plan the essay during the plenary where they need it and you could either mix abilities in the pairing during the lesson starter or keep more able with each other, giving you opportunities to help the different abilities more individually and tailored to their needs.

**Make it harder!**
More able students should write in detail about at least ten jobs. If they have time, some could produce a wall chart for the classroom.

# Women and the First World War

On 4 August 1914, World War I broke out. Two days later, the NUWSS said it was suspending all political activity until the war was over. On 10 August the government announced it was releasing all Suffragettes from prison. The WSPU agreed to stop campaigning and help Britain win the war. Women who had marched, heckled, attacked and generally caused trouble for the government in their attempts to get the vote immediately pulled together, organizing, nursing and taking jobs that men couldn't do while they were away fighting. The number of women employed increased from just over 3 million in July 1914 to nearly 5 million in January 1918.

With a partner, research the jobs that women did to contribute to the war effort.

# 8 The causes of the First World War (1)

**Introduction:** These two lessons will enable students to investigate some causes of World War I. Most will have studied issues of World War I at Key Stage 3, so there will be some overlap.

**Aims and outcomes:** At the end of the lessons, all students will recognize that the war occurred through a series of avoidable events and reactions. Most will understand Germany's position at the time. Some will appreciate contemporary European powers' viewpoints.

**Starter Lesson 1 (10 minutes):** Explain that essentially, World War I was caused by the murder of the Archduke Franz Ferdinand in June 1914. Six weeks later, many European countries were involved in a war that ultimately caused 10 million deaths. Underlying reasons had existed for years before, including nationalism, imperialism, militarism and alliances. An information sheet is online for display. Make sure that everyone understands these points. You could give them a mini-test or put them in groups to research each area and then present their findings to the class. Or select a few students to explain one aspect to class, others to explain another aspect and so on.

**Main phase, Lesson 1 (35 minutes):** Based on the information they have just received and discussed, and using whatever resources you have available, give students the following tasks.

1. Make a mind map to illustrate the underlying causes of the First World War.
2. Draw a map of Europe in 1914 to show examples of nationalism, imperialism, militarism and alliances in each country.
3. Now add the information from your map of Europe to your mind map.

**Main phase, Lesson 2 (40 minutes):** In pairs, students are to work out and explain the following. They should write in full sentences and use whatever resources are available to them:

1. Why several European countries formed alliances.
2. How the Franco-Prussian War of 1870 affected the French/German relationship.
3. How some of the four long-term causes helped to increase the likelihood of war.
4. Which of the long-term causes was the greatest threat to peace?

**Plenary, Lesson 1 (10 minutes):** Ask students to remain in their pairs and conduct a debate between them about their findings.

**Plenary, Lesson 2 (20 minutes):** Broaden the last lesson's debate so they all discuss their findings and beliefs with each other about the causes of World War I.

**Suggestion for homework (5 minutes):** Students should write up their findings from the lessons, using full sentences. The mind map and European map should also be completed.

**Make it easier!**
Less able students might only be able to complete Part 1 on their worksheets in the lesson.

**Make it harder!**
More able students could speak to the class of their findings at the start of the second lesson.

# The causes of the First World War (1)

## Part 1 (Lesson 1)

Basing your work on what you have been learning and using various available resources:

1. Make a mind map to illustrate the underlying causes of the First World War.
2. Draw a map of Europe in 1914 to show examples of nationalism, imperialism, militarism and alliances in each country.
3. Now add the information from your map of Europe to your mind map.

## Part 2 (Lesson 2)

With a partner, work out and explain the following in your exercise book. Write in full sentences and use a variety of resources:

1. Why several European countries formed alliances.
2. How the Franco-Prussian War of 1870 affected the relationship between France and Germany.
3. How some of the four long-term causes helped to increase the likelihood of war.
4. Which of the long-term causes was the greatest threat to peace.

**Useful resources**

http://www.bbc.co.uk/history/historic_figures/bismarck_otto_von.shtml
http://www.firstworldwar.com/bio/bismarck.htm
http://www.bbc.co.uk/history/historic_figures/wilhelm_kaiser_ii.shtml
http://www.firstworldwar.com/bio/wilhelmii.htm
http://www.ww1-propaganda-cards.com/sarajevo_murder.html
http://www.worldwar1.com/index.html

- It is useful for students to have some background on Kaiser Wilhelm (his grandmother was Queen Victoria; cousin King George V; born with a withered arm and possible brain damage; he was energetic and enthusiastic, but unpredictable; he had a cold family background and was ambitious for Germany) and Otto von Bismarck (from the Prussian aristocracy; changed from being an atheist to being very religious; heavy drinker in his youth; also known as the 'Iron Chancellor' as founder and first chancellor of the German Empire; great diplomat, but also extremely ambitious for Germany)
- All students should investigate how and why each country built up their armies and navies – was the arms race justified? Individual governments said that it was to prevent war, but in reality it caused serious financial difficulties for all governments involved.
- European Military spending and the size of their armies, 1913–14:

| Country | Soldiers | Money spent in millions |
|---|---|---|
| Italy | 750,000 | 10,000,000 |
| Russia | 1,250,000 | 15,500,000 |
| Austria | 750,000 | 22,500,000 |
| Germany | 8,250,000 | 60,000,000 |
| France | 1,500,000 | 40,000,000 |
| Britain | 750,000 | 50,000,000 |

# The causes of the First World War (2)

**Introduction:** This lesson considers the events that triggered the First World War, helping students to establish and understand the key figures.

**Aims and outcomes:** At the end of the lesson, all students will have studied the tensions that led to World War I. Most will recognize the strains that had been building for years across Europe and some will have clear views about which relationship was the greatest source of tension.

**Starter (10 minutes):** Remind the class about the tensions in Europe leading up to 1914 (some are in Lesson 8, including nationalism, imperialism, militarism, the Triple Alliance and the Entente). Students should list reasons for conflict between the European nations at the turn of the twentieth century. There is a list of some causes of tension in the lead up to the war online that you might like to display during or after the students have listed all the reasons they can think of.

**Main phase (35 minutes):** Students are to create a table, showing the alliances that were made between various European countries between 1879 and 1914. These are listed online and you might like to display this once they've made their tables, or have copies to hand out to those struggling. It is up to you whether they draw the table in their books by hand or produce them on the computer, and they can choose how they design them. Discuss the alliances and show a map (available online) or present the online PowerPoint to clarify the situation.

**Plenary (10 minutes):** Ask the class to close their books and turn over their task sheets. A hands-up session now for answers:

1. What is an alliance?
2. Which countries were allied by the Triple Alliance?
3. Which countries were allied by the Triple Entente?
4. Why was Germany annoyed by imperialism?
5. Which armies had increased in size between 1870 and 1914?
6. Why were the two crises important factors?

**Suggestion for homework (5 minutes):** Using numbers or bullet points, students should list events leading up to World War I. There is a prompt list of other things to research that they may not have covered yet on the task sheet, including the Austrian ultimatum to Serbia, Russian mobilization to support Serbia, Germany invading France via Belgium, and Britain avoiding commitment until the German invasion of Belgium, which broke the 1839 Treaty of London.

**Make it easier!**
Less able students might need advice on how to plan their tables and more reading time.

**Make it harder!**
Ask more able students who finish early to answer (in rough) the following questions:

1. How did imperialism contribute towards Germany's increasing anger with Britain and France?
2. Why was nationalism an important factor?

# The causes of the First World War (2)

## Part 1

Read some of the causes of tensions building in Europe

## Part 2

Using the information you have been given and any other resources you have, create a table showing the alliances that were made between various European countries between 1879 and 1914. Choose how you divide and plan your table. Suggestions:

| | | |
|---|---|---|
| | | |
| | | |
| | | |

| | |
|---|---|
| | |
| | |
| | |
| | |

| | | | |
|---|---|---|---|
| | | | |
| | | | |

**Homework:** Using numbers or bullet points, list events leading up to World War I. Here is a list of other things to research:

- The Austrian ultimatum to Serbia, which would have meant the virtual end of Serbian independence.
- Russian mobilization to support Serbia, resulting in Germany declaring war on Russia.
- Germany also declaring war on France and invading France via Belgium.
- Britain avoiding commitment until the German invasion of Belgium, which broke the 1839 Treaty of London (where European countries promised not to invade Belgium).

# 10 Long- and short-term causes of World War I

**Introduction:** This lesson allows students to consider the long- and short-term causes of the war.

**Aims and outcomes:** At the end of the lesson, all students will be able to explain the different types of causes that contributed to the outbreak of hostilities in 1914. Most students will recognize which had long-term effects and which had short-term effects and some students will be aware of the underlying repercussions that had started over 50 years before the outbreak of World War I.

**Starter (10 minutes):** Remind students that the First World War broke out in 1914. Part of its causes came from the alliance systems and the crises that arose in Morocco and the Balkans. The rivalry between the alliances led countries to increase their armed forces and they developed war plans. The tensions caused by these alliances and crises led to the assassination of Franz Ferdinand, which triggered the war plans and led to the start of the War. In small groups, students are to research and individually draw their own mind maps, entitled 'The causes of the First World War'. They should include the tensions and other conflicts that were building before the war. Make sure that they recognize which of these were long-term or short-term. They should include the alliances, the Balkan wars, the Moroccan crisis, colonial rivalries, nationalism, imperialism and so on.

**Main phase (35 minutes):** Going over all they have learned on the subject so far and using any resources available, each student should write an essay entitled 'Why the Sarajevo assassination triggered World War I'. Students should use their mind maps and previous work undertaken on this subject. You might wish to write pointers on the board as well, such as Austria's concerns about Serbia, tensions between countries, the arms race and the alliances between countries.

**Plenary (10 minutes):** Discuss with the class whether or not they feel that Germany was responsible for starting the war. Explain that, even now, no one can agree on this. Ask:

1. Was Germany entirely to blame?
2. Was Germany partly to blame, but other countries also responsible?
3. Were all the countries involved to blame?
4. Was no one to blame – was a war inevitable anyway?

What evidence do they have? Make sure they can explain the reasons for their viewpoints.

**Suggestion for homework (5 minutes):** Students should write a short passage explaining their point of view from the plenary; in other words: Who was responsible for starting the war?

**Make it easier!**
Make sure that any facts on the board, displays or handouts are clear. If necessary, give further help with essay planning and ask more able students to reiterate facts you have covered.

**Make it harder!**
More able students might still need reminding about the need to include as many detailed facts as possible. An excellent website is:

http://www.schoolhistory.co.uk

# Long- and short-term causes of World War I

## Part 1

The violent death of the Archduke and his wife formed a vital link in the long chain of events that led to what became the First World War. Fill in the spaces below.

The chain of events that led to the First World War included:

- Serb nationalists murdered the Austrian Archduke on_______________(date).
- Austria–Hungary was a powerful empire that feared it could be split if it gave in to ____________.
- By 1913, Bosnia had grown. Thousands of ________ lived there. They wanted Bosnia to break with Austria–Hungary and become part of ___________.
- Europe's complex ___________ system meant that all the great powers were dragged into war.

## Part 2

Think about all you have learned on the subject so far. Look back over all you have written about the alliances and other elements leading to war and using any resources available, plan and write an essay entitled 'Why the Sarajevo assassination triggered World War I'.

### Points for consideration

- Do you think that the alliances tying Europe's great powers together were the reasons for war?
- Which countries would have been keen for war?
- What did they want?
- Who had the largest armies and what was the history of their relationships? (For instance, France had lost the Franco-Prussian war against Germany in 1871).

**Planning your essay:** Write down all the links you can in the chain of events and then decide which causes were short-term and which were long-term. Consider tensions between countries and ambitions of individual countries.

# 11 The Schlieffen Plan

**Introduction:** This lesson looks in some detail at the Schlieffen Plan and aims to help students to understand further some of the events that led to World War I.

**Aims and outcomes:** At the end of the lesson, all students will understand what the Schlieffen Plan was and why it was unsuccessful. Most students will be aware of the assumptions that meant it was flawed from the start and some students will also recognize that any plan with no alternative tactic would be vulnerable.

**Starter (10–15 minutes):** Show the class a map of Europe in 1914, such as:

http://www.nationalarchives.gov.uk/pathways/firstworldwar/maps/map_images/Europe1914.gif

Then introduce the Schlieffen Plan to the class, either by referring them to a website or book (e.g. http://www.spartacus.schoolnet.co.uk/FWWschlieffenP.htm or *GCSE History: Student Workbook: Modern World History, 1900–49*, by Geoff Layton and Nick Dyer, published by Philip Allen, 2006). Or you could just display the background information on the Schlieffen Plan found online.

**Main phase (35 minutes):** Students are to write an essay entitled: 'Was the Schlieffen Plan the cause of World War I?' They will need to plan this carefully so, first of all, sit them in small groups to discuss their planning for 5–10 minutes, but they need to research and write their essays individually. Explain that all essays need a beginning, middle and end and they should include several points that answer the question as well as facts or evidence that underpin their points. Before they start, ask them to consider what the title is asking them to write about. In this case, it is asking them to write about how the Schlieffen Plan affected other countries and possibly helped to trigger World War I. They need to show that they understand what happened in Europe because of the Schlieffen Plan, but also what might have happened anyway, without it, and to make sure their points, evidence and explanations are clear all the way through.

**Plenary (10 minutes):** Discuss why the Schlieffen Plan failed. Talk about timing and battle plans and in what ways the Germans miscalculated. Find out who has uncovered some useful information in their essay planning. Who is having difficulties? What progress have students made? Are there any particular areas that they need to find out?

**Suggestion for homework (5 minutes):** Most students will need to complete their essays started in class, but anyone who has finished the essay should research one of the following: Kaiser Wilhelm II; Tsar Nicholas or Emperor Franz-Joseph of Austria. They should find out why their chosen person was a weak leader.

**Make it easier!**
Less able students might need more guidance in their preparation and planning of the essay. You could put less able students in groups with more able students for this, or give those students who need it a list of websites or subject areas to research.

**Make it harder!**
More able students should draw a map with their essays showing Germany, Britain, Belgium and France, marking on the directions of the armies in different colours, one per country.

# The Schlieffen Plan

You are going to write an essay entitled: 'Was the Schlieffen Plan the cause of World War I?' To plan this, you need to sit in small groups to discuss your planning for 5–10 minutes. Ask each other what you think will help you to create a clear and detailed essay, although you will ultimately be researching and writing your essay individually. All essays need a beginning, middle and end and you must include facts or evidence that answers the question and underpins your points. The title is asking you to write about how the Schlieffen Plan affected other countries and possibly helped to trigger World War I. You need to show that you understand what happened in Europe because of the Schlieffen Plan, but also what might have happened anyway, without it. Make sure your points, evidence and explanations are clear all the way through. Plan your essay in rough before you write it neatly in your exercise book or type and print it on paper.

# 12 Rivals and enemies

**Introduction:** This lesson helps students to look deeper into the alliances and rivalries between nations before the outbreak of the First World War and to work out the chain of events that triggered the conflict.

**Aims and outcomes:** At the end of the lesson, all students will understand the series of events that led to the First World War. Most students will be able to work out the chronological occurrences and knock-on effects of many of these events and some students will be aware of the particular issues that caused the greatest reverberations.

**Starter (10 minutes):** Show your class a map of Europe in 1914 and compare the size of the empire of Austria–Hungary with other countries. Explain that it was so huge that many different races populated it, including Germans, Czechs, Croats, Slovenes and Serbs and the Austrian emperor ruled over it all. In the online resources you will find a PowerPoint presentation with background information on Franz Ferdinand that you might like to use here.

**Main phase (40 minutes):** Now they know about the alliances and a bit about Austria–Hungary and Serbia/Bosnia, put students in groups of six to nine to work out the chain of events. Two or three in each group should research and make a timeline of events leading up to the war; two or three others should write down the different issues that led to the war, including alliances such as the Triple Entente and the alliance of the Central Powers. The last two or three should research and make notes about each of the first countries involved in the war: Austria–Hungary, Germany, France, Russia and Britain. After 10–15 minutes, everyone in each group should work together, using their research to plot events and occurrences in order of occurrence. They must work out causes and links and plot it all on a large sheet of paper to present to the rest of the class. In their presentations, they should explain why they arranged it in that way. This will help them to clarify the causes of the war and also the chain of events that led to the conflict.

**Plenary (10 minutes):** Could World War I have been avoided? Ask the class this in the light of their investigations during this lesson and invite intelligent responses.

**Suggestion for homework (5 minutes):** Individually, students should make their own chart or poster in their exercise books or on paper, showing the chain of events that led to the war.

**Make it easier!**

It might be helpful to mix abilities within groups. If not, you might need to give less able students some key words and suggestions for resources that they could use for research.

**Make it harder!**

More able students could produce posters to go with their charts to aid their presentations.

# Rivals and enemies

## Part 1

You are going to work in a group to work out the chain of events leading to World War I. Once you are in your group of six, decide who will do what. You will be working in pairs on separate sheets of paper.

- Two people in the group should research and make a timeline of events leading up to the war.
- Two others should write down the different issues that led to the war, including the various alliances, such as the Triple Entente and the alliance of the Central Powers.
- Two others in the group should research and write clear notes about each of the first countries involved in the war: Austria–Hungary, Germany, France, Russia and Britain. Make notes about what reasons each country had for resentment towards others.

If your group is larger, work in threes or fours on each task. When you are ready, use the timeline and the information about each country to work out how each reason links with others and on another sheet of paper, rewrite and/or arrange all your information on a large sheet of paper to make a display to present to the rest of the class.

## Part 2

Towards the end of the lesson or at the beginning of the next lesson, you will present your charts of information to the rest of the class, so make sure that you are clear about why you have reached your conclusions about the importance of events and that the rest of the class can see what you have done. In your presentation you need to explain why you have arranged your findings as you have. This should help you to clarify the causes of the war and the chain of events that led to the conflict. It is fine if another group convinces you to change your mind, as long as you are clear at the end!

# 13 British society and World War I

**Introduction:** This lesson introduces students to the mood and attitude of British civilians at the start of the First World War; how the government's propaganda perpetuated this and how the war affected everybody's lives.

**Aims and outcomes:** At the end of the lesson, all students will understand the reasons behind the propaganda put out by the British government to encourage civilians to enlist. Most students will recognize the difficulties the government faced and some students will be aware of the contradiction between ideology and actuality.

**Starter (10 minutes):** Ask the class how they think many people in Britain felt at the beginning of the First World War. Remind them that they had never experienced such a war and so to them, the idea of fighting for one's country was something to be excited about; they didn't think of death, maiming, killing, capture or struggling to survive in dreadful conditions. Without firsthand knowledge, war was not a reality but an ideal and patriotic fervour ran high. Ask: how was the war portrayed? Show students a selection of propaganda images from the First World War. There are links to some images online.

Give the class some time to look at the images and consider them and then ask them some questions. There are six suggested questions online that you might like to display on the whiteboard.

**Main phase (35 minutes):** Everyone should read their task sheets, then pair them up and ask them to answer the questions on their sheets, using whatever resources you have. Answers should be thorough (which is why they're being allowed to research in pairs).

**Plenary (10 minutes):** Have a brief discussion with the entire class about what students have discovered this lesson. In the last 5–10 minutes, students should begin planning an essay entitled 'The impact of World War I on civilian life'. This will be an opportunity for them to think about it and raise any questions about the essay.

**Suggestion for homework (5 minutes):** The essay should be planned and, depending on the time your students have, even started for next lesson. Students should make notes of anything they are finding difficult to discuss.

**Make it easier!**

The way in which this lesson is structured should give a variety of support to a wide variety of abilities and learning styles. You may need to give further assistance to less able students, in terms of showing them helpful resources and discussing the questions in the main part of the lesson in more depth.

**Make it harder!**

More able students should research the 'Home Front' during the war and write a short passage in rough about it.

# British society and World War I

Once the war had started, the British government had to take control, not only of the troops fighting away from home, but also of the civilians who remained behind. Most people believed that the war would be over by Christmas and, in the first six weeks, half a million men enlisted into the British armed forces. When the war continued with no end in sight and massive casualties, enthusiasm waned. The government had to keep enlisting volunteers and so it began a huge propaganda campaign, trying to tempt more people to fight for their country. One of the ways they did this was to encourage extreme anti-German views.

With a partner, find detailed answers to the following questions. The answers will need to be thorough and written clearly and carefully. Use a variety of resources to make sure that your answers are as unbiased as possible. Write your answers in your exercise book – each answer should be at least one paragraph in length.

1. How did the government promote the war to civilians at home – why, what did it want to achieve and was it successful?
2. The *Defence of the Realm Acts* – what were they, when were they and how did they work?
3. The introduction of conscription – when and what was this, how did it work and why was it introduced?
4. Why there were food shortages during the war and what was done to help this problem?
5. What was the Propaganda Bureau, what did it do and what did it become?

# 14 Trench warfare

**Introduction:** This lesson helps students to understand the conditions in the World War I trenches and to appreciate the government's stance in keeping the reality from those at home.

**Aims and outcomes:** At the end of the lesson, all students will understand some details of what conditions were like in the trenches. Most students will realize how unexpected the situation was for everyone and the shock and horror that most young men would have faced without prior conditioning. Some students will understand why the government did not want civilians at home to know about the conditions as they needed to both keep up morale and enlist more men.

**Starter (10 minutes):** Begin the lesson with a discussion. What do students think the mood was like in Britain in 1914 when the war first began? How do they think people felt about sending their sons, brothers, cousins, uncles and friends off to war? Without prior experience of such a war, most people had a romanticized view of war. Would the enthusiasm have been so high if the same thing happened today? If not, why not? Give them a list of words to explain – hands-up responses and quick one-word answers are enough: Allies, Volunteer, Enlist, Civilians and Trench (these are online in case you want to display them on the board).

**Main phase (40 minutes):** Ask students if they know what trench warfare was and what life was like for soldiers in the trenches. There is an information sheet online that you might like to display. Then, in pairs and in 10 minutes, they are to find out what the following words mean: Waterlogged, Duck boards, Trench foot, Dugouts, Front-line, Artillery, No-man's land and Snipers (there is a document online in case you would like to put these on the board). Again, hands-up responses are required. Remaining in pairs, using any resources available, students are to research life in the trenches. They are to plan an article between them, imagining that they are journalists who have managed to find out and tell the truth in a newspaper article. To start them off, you could show them some contemporary cartoons, such as those by Bruce Bairnsfather provided online. Discuss the humour in these images and why they were trying to make light of the situation. Make sure your students recognize the shock and strangeness of the trenches to the many young men once they were out there. Explain that many people at home did not realize what life was really like in the trenches and the government did not want them to in order to a) keep up morale and b) receive more volunteers into the armed forces. There is further background information online that you might like to project onto the whiteboard while they plan their articles.

**Plenary (5 minutes):** Ask students to volunteer to read out a paragraph from their reports. What particularly interesting facts have they uncovered to share with the rest of the class?

**Suggestion for homework (5 minutes):** Students are to complete their articles about life in the trenches.

**Make it easier!**
Less able students might try to skim over the surface, so you might need to advise them on some of the areas they should research, including underground warfare, tunnelling, look-out posts and so on. You could advise the class to consider the five senses as they write and explain in their articles how each was affected.

**Make it harder!**
More able students should recognize the need to include detailed information about tactics and daily activities in trenches.

# Trench warfare

In pairs, find out what the following words mean and put your hands up to answer – no calling out:

1. Waterlogged
2. Duck boards
3. Trench foot
4. Dugouts
5. Front-line
6. Artillery
7. No-man's land
8. Snipers

Remaining with your partner, research the topic: 'What was life like in the trenches?' Imagine you are a journalist who has managed to find out and tell the truth in a newspaper article. Help each other to research and plan your article together. Use whatever resources are available.

# 15 The Battle of the Somme

**Introduction:** This lesson helps students to understand why the First World War was spent mainly at deadlock and it was virtually impossible for either side to break through. Although each side fought hard, for most of the war, nobody made much progress.

**Aims and outcomes:** At the end of the lesson, all students will recognize Britain's pledge to Belgium and why it had to become involved. Most students will be able to analyse why methods and equipment aided defence rather than attack and some students will accept that with hindsight it is easy to analyse and judge, but they will recognize how different battles occurred and resulted in deadlock.

**Starter (10 minutes):** Explain to the class that the tactics and equipment of both the Germans and their allies and the French and their allies were suited to defence, not necessarily attack, so although millions of men were killed, they would never have broken the stalemate unless something changed. Ask if anyone can explain why. You may need to elaborate if necessary, and there are some facts and figures online.

**Main phase (40 minutes):** Talk about the heavy losses during the war and how this weakened both sides – physically and morally. Explain that by November 1916, at the end of the Battle of the Somme, approximately 1.25 million men had been killed. The war had become a battle of wits – a contest to see which side could hold out the longest. Field Marshall Douglas Haig told the British government 'the nation must be taught to bear losses'. Ask the class why they think that Haig said that and what was the nation's reaction to it? Next, in small groups, everyone is to research the Battle of the Somme. They are to find out as much as possible about the events of the battle. After researching individually for about 30 minutes, students should work in groups of three to write a detailed account of the Battle of the Somme. A list of suggested websites to use for research is online, as well as some introductory information that you might like to hand out or display on the board.

**Plenary (5 minutes):** Individually, everyone should write a list of as many reasons as they can as to why the Battle of the Somme would never have gone beyond the stalemate.

**Suggestion for homework (5 minutes):** Students should imagine they are soldiers, fighting at the Battle of the Somme. They should write a diary entry for one day, explaining the events of the day.

**Make it easier!**
You might find that mixing abilities within groups helps the outcome – or you might find that it is better for your class to have less able and more able groups. Give less able groups a list of key words or phrases to look up.

**Make it harder!**
More able students could produce an illustrated essay on the Battle of the Somme for display.

# The Battle of the Somme

## Part 1

By November 1916, at the end of the Battle of the Somme, approximately 1.25 million men had been killed. The war had become a battle of wits – a contest to see which side could hold out the longest. Field Marshall Douglas Haig told the British government 'the nation must be taught to bear losses'.

Why do you think that Field Marshall Haig said that and what was the nation's reaction to it?

## Part 2

Think about your answer, then research the Battle of the Somme. In 30 minutes, find out as much as you can about the events of the battle. Then you will either choose your group or be told who you are working with, and in a group of three you are to write a detailed account of the Battle of the Somme. You should all contribute information, then work it out in a coherent short essay and type it on computer.

# 16 What caused the stalemate for most of World War I?

**Introduction:** This lesson asks students to consider the events and setbacks of the First World War and the reasons why millions of young men died, yet hardly any ground was taken by either side.

**Aims and outcomes:** At the end of the lesson, all students will realize that mistakes were made during World War I and they will recognize that a lack of knowledge was one of the reasons for these mistakes. Most students will also realize that arrogance and assumptions occurred on both sides and why there are different interpretations of many of the main battles of the war. Some students will understand many of the reasons why these were not the victories that both the commanders and civilians at home expected them to be and why stalemate was not broken in four years.

**Starter (15 minutes):** If possible, show the class a clip from *Blackadder Goes Forth*, from a few moments before they go over the top, to the end, when the shot is of the silent field as it is today. (There is a link from YouTube available online.) You could also ask a student to read an excerpt from war poetry by Wilfred Owen, Siegfried Sassoon or Rupert Brook (links provided online). Give the class a chance to digest what they have seen or heard, and discuss whether a television comedy show can be of any use to historians. Ask them if they can think of any evidence of bad leadership, human suffering and failure.

**Main phase (35 minutes):** In small groups, students are to work together to create presentations that they will perform in front of the class, showing why the First World War remained in a deadlock for four years. In their groups, they will need to research the questions on their task sheets.

If time, ask some of the groups to present their findings to the rest of the class.

**Plenary (5 minutes):** Everyone in the class should make clear notes about what they have found out about why there was stalemate during the First World War. Groups that have not presented will have to be ready to present their findings next lesson.

**Suggestion for homework (5 minutes):** Imagining that they are soldiers of World War I, students should research and write a short letter 'home' describing one of the following battles: the Somme, Verdun, Ypres, Loos or Mons. In their letters, they should consider: where the battle occurred; the events that led to it; the commands of the generals; the difficulties and methods of communication; battle conditions, such as the weather; who was involved; types of weapons used; surroundings; morale and how many casualties, plus anything else that they believe would be relevant to helping their family at home to understand the events and outcomes of the battle.

**Make it easier!**

For the homework, less able students might need a more detailed outline of the task, with some key events and issues to consider and more specifics for their research.

**Make it harder!**

More able students should present first.

# What caused the stalemate for most of World War I?

Working in a small group, you are to create a presentation for the rest of the class, showing why the First World War remained in a deadlock for four years. You will need to research:

1. Commanders' experience and expertise – what they knew about.
2. Whether the commanders cared for their soldiers and how they participated in the fighting.
3. The lack of knowledge of modern artillery and its effectiveness in killing.
4. What happened to soldiers who 'deserted'?
5. How communication between headquarters and the Front and between allies (e.g. French and British). How safe were messengers?
6. How fit or able were the soldiers?
7. Specifically, the inefficiency of the French and British shrapnel shells on the German trenches and their explosives in tunnels under the German trenches.
8. The assumptions made by Commanders and any continued mistakes made by them.

**Useful resources**

http://www.pbs.org/greatwar/chapters/ch2_overview.html
http://www.bbc.co.uk/schools/worldwarone/hq/wfront3_01.shtml
http://www.historyteacher.net/APEuroCourse/WebLinks/WebLinks-WorldWar1.htm
http://www.spartacus.schoolnet.co.uk/FWWbattles.htm

# Why was the war not over by Christmas?

**Introduction:** This lesson helps students to consider why people believed that the war would be over by Christmas 1914 and why, in the event, it lasted for four years.

**Aims and outcomes:** At the end of the lesson, all students will be able to analyse and explain why the war was not over by the end of 1914. Most students will understand how and why new methods of warfare came as a shock to generals and commanders and some students will be aware of the pressure that the government was under to keep the public believing that the conflict would be short-lived.

**Starter (10 minutes):** Tell the class that when soldiers volunteered to fight in the summer and autumn of 1914, they were eager to fight, partly because everyone believed the war would be over by Christmas. Ask the class:

a. What made people think this?
b. Why did the war last for four years, rather than four months?

Students should discuss this among themselves for a couple of minutes and then share their responses in a class discussion.

**Main phase (40 minutes):** Working in pairs, students are to imagine that television was around in 1914 and write a script for a TV news report, explaining what was happening at the Front in 1914 and why the war might not be over by Christmas after all. Some key areas to consider are on the task sheets as well. They should write their news reports as scripts, and think about what images they are going to show alongside the news report.

**Plenary (5 minutes):** Ask students to share where they have found out relevant facts. Do they have any sources and resources to share? Students should make a note of valuable resources.

**Suggestion for homework (5 minutes):** Students should continue writing their scripts and/or planning to present to the class, either as a PowerPoint or as a live presentation.

**Make it easier!**
As many students will not be able to work with their partners for homework, it would be helpful if you can give them opportunities to work together during any breaks, lunch breaks or after school. If necessary, you might need to give extra guidance to some less able students with their research.

**Make it harder!**
If you have the facilities, students could actually film or record their television programme. If facilities are not available, then they could produce neat and colourful storyboards for class display.

# Why was the war not over by Christmas?

With a partner, imagine that television was around in 1914 and write a script for a TV news report, explaining what was happening at the Front in 1914 and why the war might not be over by Christmas after all. Here are some key areas to consider as you research:

- Successes and setbacks of battles and plans.
- Important battles that were fought and why.
- Injuries and deaths – the extent and the shock of it all.
- New lessons to be learned about warfare.
- The spirits of the troops – good or bad? How did they keep up morale?

Write your news report as a script, so divide the page or pages into two columns. On the right-hand side, write the speech and on the left-hand side, describe what images you will be showing:

| **Speech, music and sound effects** | **Images** |
|---|---|
| | |

# 18 To what extent did conditions change between 1914 and 1918?

**Introduction:** This lesson asks students to consider the events and changes that occurred during the First World War. It helps them to understand how and why conditions changed during the four years of the war.

**Aims and outcomes:** At the end of the lesson, all students will understand some of the global consequences of World War I. Most students will understand why so many countries entered the war and some students will understand how the Russian Revolution and the entry of the United States affected the course and outcome of the war.

**Starter (15 minutes):** Put students in small groups or pairs and ask them to write a short quiz about some of the battles of World War I. After 10 minutes, the groups or pairs should swap their quizzes with another group. 5 minutes to answer!

**Main phase (35 minutes):** Give the students some background on events that occurred between 1914 and 1918. There is an information sheet online if you'd like to use this. Then the class is to find out why different nations joined certain sides, in particular the Russians joining the Austria–Hungarians and the Germans and the Americans joining Britain and France. Working in pairs, students are to make charts showing the stance of different countries in the war. They will need to work out how best to show this and to include when each country joined or whether it remained neutral. Key information on the alliances (online) should be read and displayed to make sure everyone is clear.

**Plenary (5 minutes):** Go around the class, asking students how many countries they have managed to list. Select a few of them to volunteer one of their countries and see if others in the class had the same result.

**Suggestion for homework (5 minutes):** Everyone should answer the multiple-choice questions on their task sheets.

**Make it easier!**
Consider mixed ability pairings or give less able students more guidance in terms of specific books or websites to look at.

**Make it harder!**
Still with their partners, more able students could write an account of the trenches from the point of view of a young soldier.

# To what extent did conditions change between 1914 and 1918?

You are going to find out why different nations joined certain sides, in particular the Russians joining the Austrian–Hungarians and the Germans and the Americans joining Britain and France. With a partner, produce charts showing the stance of different countries in the war. Work out how best to show this and include when each country joined or whether it remained neutral.

**Homework quiz:** The stalemate on the Western Front lasted for so long because:

1. It was very difficult for men and horses to charge quickly because 'No-man's land' usually consisted of
   a. Deep mud and barbed wire
   b. Fine sand and cement
   c. Paving stones and hay fields
2. Weapons used in the First World War were better suited for defending than for attacking. As attacking soldiers charged across 'No-man's land' they were mowed down by
   a. Tanks and other army vehicles
   b. Machine-gun fire or blown up by land mines
   c. Tractors and combine harvesters
3. The generals were not used to fighting this type of warfare. The only tactic they could think of was to
   a. Tell men to hide in the trenches
   b. Fight from the skies
   c. Keep sending men across 'No-man's land'
4. Before an attack, enemy trenches were bombarded with heavy artillery but instead of killing many of them, this just warned the enemy that an attack was coming, losing
   a. The element of surprise
   b. The battle
   c. The will to live

# Section C International relations (1)

# 19 The peace treaties

**Introduction:** This lesson introduces students to the peace treaties that were signed at the end of World War I. It will underpin their knowledge about the viewpoints of some of the countries involved. With this understanding and knowledge, they will question whether or not the treaties were fair.

**Aims and objectives:** At the end of the lesson, all students will understand why peace treaties were drawn up at the end of World War I. Most students will have been able to consider the impact of the terms on many countries involved and some students will recognize some of both the broader difficulties of making treaties to meet all needs.

**Starter (10 minutes):** Show the class a map of Europe at the end of the First World War. Divide them into ten small groups and tell each that they represent a country: France, Germany, Austria, UK, Italy, Russia, Belgium, the Netherlands, Spain and the US. Ask each group to jot down on whose side they fought during the war. In their groups they are to study the map of Europe, consider the devastation the war had on the land and the people and consider their own positions as individual countries. Each group must write a list of about ten things they would agree to as the way to peace and reconstruction of relationships between countries and the rebuilding of those countries that were devastated during the war.

**Main phase (40 minutes): Part 1:** Spokespeople from each group should list their wishes for their own peace treaties. Write the main points on the board. You will need to act as chair while the groups work things out between them. Spend no more than 15 minutes on this – don't allow them to drag it out! It is merely an exercise to show them how difficult it was to work out fair peace plans.

**Part 2:** Give the class a bit of background on the 'Big Three' and the Treaty of Versailles. There is a 'background information' sheet on the Big Three online and details about the Treaty of Versailles on the task sheet. In the groups they have been working in, ask the students to work out what they think were the most important issues of the Versailles Peace Treaty. Students are then, in their own words, to explain the Treaty of Versailles, in particular, what Germany had to do.

**Plenary (5 minutes):** Run over the main points of the lesson and make sure that everyone understands. Students should make a simple list on the board of Germany's obligations.

**Suggestion for homework (5 minutes):** All students are to write an account, answering the following question: was the Treaty of Versailles harsh on Germany?

**Make it easier!**
Less able students might need your attention during the activities of this lesson, while more able students might work more intently if they are given plenty of resources and independence.

**Make it harder!**
More able students could discuss and work out another way that peace and reconciliation might have been made.

# The peace treaties

The first 26 clauses of the Versailles Peace Treaty dealt with organization of the League of Nations, but the essence of the rest of it was:

1. The following land was taken away from Germany:
   Alsace–Lorraine (given to France), Eupen and Malmedy (given to Belgium), Northern Schleswig (given to Denmark), Hultschin (given to Czechoslovakia), West Prussia, Posen and Upper Silesia (given to Poland), the Saar, Danzig and Memel were put under the control of the League of Nations and the people of these regions would be allowed to vote to stay in Germany or not.
2. The League of Nations also took control of Germany's overseas colonies. Germany had to return land taken in the Treaty of Brest-Litovsk back to Russia. Some of this land was made into new states: Estonia, Lithuania and Latvia. An enlarged Poland also received some of this land.
3. Germany's army was reduced to 100,000 men and they were not allowed tanks. Neither was Germany allowed an air force. It could also have only six naval ships and no submarines.
4. The west of the Rhineland and 50 km east of the river Rhine was made into a demilitarized zone (DMZ). No German soldier or weapon was allowed into this zone. The Allies were to keep an army on the west bank of the Rhine for 15 years.
5. Germany was forbidden to unite with Austria in an attempt to keep her economic potential to a minimum.
6. Germany had to admit full responsibility for starting the war. This became known as the 'War Guilt Clause'.
7. In accepting full responsibility for the war, the Germans were therefore also responsible for all the war damage. Therefore, Germany had to pay reparations or payments back to countries such as France and Belgium to pay for the damage done to both countries by the war. The figure was not set at Versailles but it was decided upon later. The amount was eventually put at £6,600 million – an enormous amount of money and far more than Germany could afford.
8. The loss of important industrial territory was a harsh setback to any attempts by Germany to rebuild its economy. Valuable resources would be lost to the Germans because of vital land taken away. Along with the reparations, it seemed to the Germans that the Allies were trying to bankrupt their country.

Work out what you think were the most important issues of the Versailles Peace Treaty. Now, in your own words, in your exercise book, explain the Treaty of Versailles, in particular, what Germany had to do.

# 20 The Treaty of Versailles (1)

**Introduction:** This lesson helps students to understand some of the problems that delegates faced when meeting to deal with the problem of peace in Paris in 1919. With further knowledge, they will be able to decide whether the Paris Peace Conference made a sensible settlement.

**Aims and outcomes:** At the end of this lesson, all students should be aware of at least four problems that representatives of each country faced when drawing up the peace treaties. Most students will understand which of their problems was the most difficult to sort out and some students will understand the different opinions of the 'Big Three'.

**Starter (10 minutes):** Show the class an image of the painting by William Orpen in 1919 of *The Signing of the Treaty of Versailles* (available online). Discuss what is happening. Can they see the man in front of the table, with his head down? Point out how all the other stern-looking men are watching him. Explain that politicians gathered in the Palace of Versailles' renowned Hall of Mirrors on 28 June 1919, exactly five years after the Archduke Franz Ferdinand had been assassinated. This painting is of that gathering. All the powerful politicians are watching in silence as the German representatives entered the room and walked slowly across to the long table where they all sat, and signed the peace treaty. How must it have felt to be those men? How did the other men who were watching feel? Tell students that, for the next few minutes, they are going to imagine they are one of the people in that room, of a nationality that you are going to give them. (There does not have to be an even number of nationalities). Ask students to consider the issues of the day. What would they want the peace treaty to say? Pick people around the room to answer those questions.

**Main phase (40 minutes):** Read the task sheet and choose three students to 'be' Woodrow Wilson, Georges Clemenceau and David Lloyd George. Then conduct the meeting of these three important people, plus other diplomats and politicians. Let them lead the meeting where possible, but be ready to steer them on to the right course. Remind them that everyone is trying to work towards long-term peace. Remind them too to consider the four problems on the task sheet and everyone is to decide which think is the most important – and how will they solve it? The whole class should work out a list of resolutions to solve the problems of the war.

**Plenary (5 minutes):** What solution has the class come up with? How have the three politicians resolved their wants and beliefs? What list of requirements and actions have they made? Does anyone want to change anything?

**Suggestion for homework (5 minutes):** Students should first of all write down the main problems that politicians faced after the war and, secondly, the main ideas of each of the Big Three.

**Make it easier!**
If any students seem not to be concentrating or losing the thread of the discussion, slow down or stop the debate and ask someone in the class to explain what has just happened. Make sure that everyone makes notes during the lesson, as they will need these for their homework.

**Make it harder!**
Ask more able students to write a diary entry of the peace settlement from the point of view of one of the Big Three.

# The Treaty of Versailles (1)

When they met in Paris, the politicians faced many problems. Here are the four main ones:

1. War has brought terrible destruction in particular to land and buildings in France. How can it all be repaired?
2. A consequence of the war is that more countries than ever want to rule themselves and to escape from empires, which try to control large parts of the land.
3. In 1917, Communists took over Russia and their ideas are becoming popular with many who also believe that the poor should take power from the wealthy.
4. Twenty million lives have been lost. How can future wars be prevented?

Your teacher is choosing three people in the class to 'be' Woodrow Wilson, Georges Clemenceau and David Lloyd George. These three important people are going to meet, while the rest of the class represents other diplomats and politicians. Whatever role you are taking, remember that everyone is trying to work towards long-term peace – you have just emerged from the most horrific war ever known. Out of the four problems above, which do you think is the most important – and how will you solve it? Between you, work out a list of resolutions to the problems of the war.

# 21 The Treaty of Versailles (2)

**Introduction:** This lesson looks fairly closely at the Treaty of Versailles and helps students to understand why it was so severe. It introduces some of the background to the treaty; the problems involved in its design and the problems and issues its implementation caused.

**Aims and objectives:** At the end of the lesson, all students will understand some of the details of the Treaty of Versailles and the reasons the demands were made. Most students will realize the detrimental effects this had on Germany and some students will be aware how the conditions were created for subjective reasons rather than being an equal and objective contract.

**Starter (10 minutes):** Display 'The three odd ones out' online document or print copies off and give them out to the class. Ask students which three were *not* parts of the Treaty of Versailles. Discuss the correct answers. Can they remember why certain other countries wanted certain stipulations in the Treaty? Ask students to put up their hands to give definitions for the following words:

- Republic
- Autocratic
- Democratic
- Reparation
- Inflation
- Treaty

They are included online in case you want to display them on the board.

**Main phase (35 minutes):** Give out copies of or display Woodrow Wilson's Fourteen Points and ask hand out a list of the main points of the Treaty of Versailles (there is a copy of this online). They should answer all questions on the task sheet. Questions in Part 1 can be written in note form or bullet points in rough, but questions in Part 2 must be written in detail in their exercise books.

**Plenary (10 minutes):** Show the class a map of Europe at the end of the war. Ask them:

a. Should Alsace–Lorraine have been given back to France or kept by Germany?
b. Why was Germany forbidden to put any soldiers in the Rhineland?
c. Who should have had the Saarland – France or Germany?
d. Should Austria–Hungary have been allowed to continue as one country or split into two?

**Suggestion for homework (5 minutes):** Students are to find out about the Weimar Republic. What was it and why did some extremists try to overthrow it in 1919? They should write their answers in a couple of paragraphs.

**Make it easier!**
As most of this lesson is oral rather than written, some students might try to avoid participation, so you need to ask some of these individuals directly for their opinions from time to time. If you suspect that certain students are still evading involvement, give some individual assistance with the written task, and if they are being distracted, move them to another place in the room.

**Make it harder!**
More able students could make a table showing the main effects of the treaty on Germany and, in comparison, the main effects on the rest of Europe.

# The Treaty of Versailles (2)

## Part 1

Think about the following and write down bullet point answers in rough:

- Was the Treaty of Versailles fair to Germany?
- Were Germans happy with its stipulations?
- Should the German government have been allowed to discuss it first or had Germans forfeited that right by their actions in the war?
- Had all Germans wanted to surrender?
- What if some had wanted to continue fighting?
- How do you think that those Germans felt about their own governments and the governments of the countries that drew up the Treaty of Versailles?
- Why do you think there was a revolution in Germany in November 1918 and why did Kaiser Wilhelm II abdicate?

## Part 2

Looking at Woodrow Wilson's Fourteen Points and the main points of the Treaty of Versailles (from the last lesson), write answers for the following:

a. Which points are the same or very similar?

b. Why are they different from each other?

c. Why did the Germans want Wilson's Fourteen Points?

d. How helpful would it have been to allow the defeated nations to attend and discuss the conditions of the treaty?

e. Should the Germans have signed the treaty?

# 22 The Treaty of Versailles (3)

**Introduction:** Continuing to investigate the Treaty of Versailles, students will consider events in Germany, particularly the elections, and Friedrich Ebert.

**Aims and outcomes:** At the end of the lesson, all students will understand what the German people resented about the Treaty of Versailles. Most students will recognize that it was too harsh and some students will realize the long-term damage it was to cause.

**Starter (10 minutes):** In pairs, students are to work out a German timeline from October 1918 to February 1919. They must include at least ten things that happened during that time. Hints:

- Kaiser Wilhelm
- Spanish flu
- General Ludendorff
- Friedrich Ebert
- Socialists
- Spartacists
- Weimar Republic
- Communism
- Free Corps
- Sailors
- Uprisings/riots

**Main phase (35 minutes):** Discuss with the class the end of World War I – what happened in Germany? What did each of the 'Big Three' say about Germany and maintaining peace? Tell them about the Spartacist uprising and the general election four days after it (there is an online document that you might like to display or print off and hand out). Recap with students what they remember about this; how the Treaty of Versailles was drawn up and why most Germans thought that it was humiliating and unfair. Their task is to write a letter to an imaginary German newspaper of 1919, pretending that they are German citizens of that time and summarizing the main points of the treaty, asking 'is it fair?'

**Plenary (10 minutes):** Ask for some letters to be read out to the class. How have students managed? Who has conducted particularly useful research? Discuss their considered opinions – what do they think the Germans were expecting?

**Suggestion for homework (5 minutes):** Students are to write an essay entitled 'Why did the Germans hate the Treaty of Versailles so much?' In the essay, they should summarize the main points of the treaty and explain why the terms seemed so unfair to Germany. They should consider: war guilt (acceptance of blame for the war); reparations (paying compensation); military restrictions and territorial losses.

**Make it easier!**
Help less able students by giving them specific books and websites to help them with their research.

**Make it harder!**
More able students will be able to research in enough detail to produce detailed written tasks, while less able students might need further guidance from you.

# The Treaty of Versailles (3)

Remember how the Treaty of Versailles was drawn up and remember why most Germans thought it was humiliating and unfair. You are to write a letter to an imaginary German newspaper of 1919, pretending that you are German citizens of that time. Summarize the main points of the treaty and ask 'is it fair?' Consider:

- Germany having to take the blame for the war.
- Germany having to pay large reparations (the total bill was set at £6,600 million).
- Germany losing approximately 10 per cent of its industry and 15 per cent of its agricultural land, so income would drop.
- Germany's armed forces were reduced and the air force was to be disbanded.
- No German troops were allowed in Germany.
- Germany losing 13 per cent of its land, which contained about 6 million Germans.

Meanwhile, the German people believed:

- The treaty was too harsh.
- They hadn't started the war, but had been defending themselves.
- Germany had been happy and powerful before the war.

# 23 Why did the Weimar Republic face opposition between 1919 and 1923?



**Introduction:** This lesson looks at the failure of the Weimar Republic, in particular, the causes and consequences of the 'Great Inflation' of 1923.

**Aims and outcomes:** At the end of the lesson, all students will understand the main causes of the financial difficulties and other related problems in Germany after World War I and why the Weimar Republic was blamed for it all. Most students will recognize the psychological impact the Treaty of Versailles had on German society. Some students will be able to understand some detailed causes and consequences of the problems after World War I and where the Weimar Republic was at fault.

**Starter (15 minutes):** Explain that Germany became a republic in 1919 after the abdication of Kaiser William II and the country's defeat in World War I. The new government was moved to Weimar, a town far away from the capital Berlin, to escape the unrest and violence that broke out there. Because of this, the regime is often called the Weimar Republic.

Ask the class:

1. What is a republic?
2. How do they think that Germans felt about the new government?
3. Why do they think that unrest and violence broke out in Berlin?

Next, ask everyone to imagine how the majority of Germans felt. Apart from anything else, they had suffered severe food shortages just before the end of the war because of a British naval blockade. The new republican leaders made peace with the Allies, but many Germans were furious. They did not believe that their armies had been defeated and they labelled those who had made peace the 'November Criminals'. A conspiracy theory was invented and circulated – that Germany had not been defeated at all, but had been 'stabbed in the back' by various rebels within the country, including Jews and socialists. Students should write down the following key phrases and explain them briefly in their own words (these are online in case you want to display them on the board):

- Republic
- Blockade
- November Criminals
- Stab-in-the-back theory

**Main phase (35 minutes):** Give the students some background on the Weimar Republic and discuss with the students the important features of the financial situation, the reparations and public feeling. There is background information online that you can display if you choose. Everyone is to research what caused the 'Great Inflation' of 1923. Although they are researching together, each should write their own account of the causes.

**Plenary (10 minutes):** Select four groups of students to quickly look up other peace treaties and to give the rest of the class a basic outline of each:

(*continued over page 56*)

# Why did the Weimar Republic face opposition between 1919 and 1923?

What do you think?

- Did reparations ruin the German economy?
- If not, what did?

With a partner or in a small group, discuss this and then research what caused the 'Great Inflation' of 1923. Although you are researching together, write your own account of the causes in your exercise book. Consider:

- The amount of reparations – were the costs too high?
- What was the psychological impact on the people of the reparations and inflation?
- Was the Weimar Republic to blame?
- Was Kaiser Wilhelm II to blame?
- What other issues caused the financial situation?

1. Treaty of St Germain
2. Treaty of Neuilly
3. Treaty of Trianon
4. Treaty of Sèvres

Everyone should make notes.

**Suggestion for homework (5 minutes):** In a written account, students should answer *one* of the following:

a. What was the impact of the peace treaties on the other defeated nations?
b. Did the winners of the war get all they wanted from the peace treaties?
c. Were all the treaties fair?

(You could ask them to write their answers in note form and write an essay on their chosen question in a subsequent lesson).

**Make it easier!**
Spend time going around the room, talking to students and asking them if they understand the task.

**Make it harder!**
More able students could make notes on how the Weimar Republic faced opposition but survived in 1923 and the achievements of the Weimar period.

# Section D Russia

# 24 How was Russia structured at the beginning of the 20th century?

**Introduction:** This lesson helps students consider the consequential difficulties in Britain after the war.

**Aims and objectives:** At the end of the lesson, all students will be aware of the problems of class and money in Russia at the end of the nineteenth and beginning of the twentieth centuries. Most students will recognize that attitudes changed drastically after the First World War when so many young men had been killed. Some students will recognize the problems of the autocratic government and of the rise of capitalism.

**Starter (15 minutes):** Tell the class that when Nicholas II was crowned Tsar of Russia in 1894, crowds flocked to St Petersburg to cheer. There were so many people there that it was reported that 1,200 people were crushed to death. Twenty-three years later, he and his family were rounded up as prisoners and taken to an isolated house, far away from their opulent palaces.

Working in pairs and using a variety of resources, allow students 10 minutes to research briefly what had happened. After the allotted time, call out two or three pairs, to sit at the front of the room and to be questioned on the topic by the rest of the class. You will probably need to join in to stimulate students' questions and to help with responses, but where possible, refrain from helping too much and try to let them do all the work!



**Main phase (35 minutes):** Read through the information in Part 1 of the task sheet on the Tsar (this is also available online in case you would like to display it on the board). Students should then research the four things laid out in Part 2 of the task sheet. Everyone is to write an article on this in the style of a sensationalist newspaper – as if everything is happening now – they are to try and stir up readers as contemporary tabloids do. Stop the class once or twice during their activities and ask how everyone is finding the work, get them to share tips and ideas to help bring some back to focus if their concentration is slipping.

**Plenary (5 minutes):** Invite feedback on the research conducted. Ask who has anything interesting to share with the class about their findings? (Pick some if they don't willingly volunteer). How was Russia structured at the turn of the twentieth century? How hard were the lives of the peasants and how privileged were the lives of the rich? What caused the increase of the middle classes?

**Suggestion for homework (5 minutes):** Students are to write a passage explaining: 'Why did unrest in Russia occur after World War I?' They should use their findings from the lesson to help them in their responses. The passage should be at least 400 words and evidence and sources should be quoted.

**Make it easier!**
Give less able students further guidance if they appear to need it during the lesson.

**Make it harder!**
Keep an eye on more able students to make sure that they are challenging themselves enough. During the plenary, try to encourage the quieter members of the class to join in with responses.

# How was Russia structured at the beginning of the 20th century?

## Part 1

Until 1917, Russia was ruled by an autocrat ('one who rules by himself') – the Tsar. He meant well but was inefficient and kept his position by means of the secret police. He mistrusted most of his ministers and yet was incapable of carrying out the task of ruling the vast Russian empire alone. He wanted to increase Russia's colonies and encouraged Russian expansion in Manchuria, which provoked war with Japan in 1904. After being defeated, there were several strikes and riots in Russia.

## Part 2

You are to research four things:

1. Tsar Nicholas II – what kind of person was he, how did he live and what did he do while in power?
2. The Russian aristocracy – how did they live, how did they help to run the country and how much of Russia did they own?
3. Russian peasants – approximately how many were there? How did they live?
4. The capitalists – who were they, where did they come from and what did they think of other Russians?

Write an article on this in the style of a sensationalist newspaper – as if everything is happening now – try to stir up readers as many tabloids do today.

# 25 Russia divided

**Introduction:** This expands on the previous lesson: helping students to understand how divided Russia had become after the First World War and what this led to. (Students need to be made aware that in 1917 the Russians used the Julian calendar, which was 13 days behind the Gregorian calendar used by the rest of Europe. Therefore dates referring to action in Russia at this time are usually given according to the Julian calendar. Thus, the 'October Revolution' of 25 October, happened on 7 November by English reckoning).

**Aims and outcomes:** At the end of the lesson, all students will understand many of the reasons for the unrest and divided opinions among Russian people in 1917. Most students will realize why workers walked out of their jobs and why the soldiers joined them. They will understand the basics of socialism and communism. Some students will recognize that not everyone supported the Bolsheviks in 1917, which led to civil war.

**Starter (10–15 minutes):** Give the class a bit of background on post-war Russia first of all (this is available as an online resource), then ask the class:

1. Why did the soldiers refuse to fire at the demonstrators?
2. What is a demonstration?
3. What is a democratic government?
4. What is socialism?
5. What is a monarchy?

Have a short class discussion to make sure that everyone understands these points.

**Main phase (35–40 minutes):** Divide the class into five groups. Each group is to research one of the following people: Nicholas II, Rasputin, Alexander Kerensky, Vladimir Lenin or Leon Trotsky.

Each group is to prepare a presentation about the person they are researching, to present to the rest of the class in the second half of the lesson. Presentations should be no more than 5 minutes in length and information about what they should include is on the task sheet.

**Plenary (5 minutes):** Discuss the five people's lives that have been researched and talked about in the lesson. Establish their importance in the unrest and divided opinions in Russia.

**Suggestion for homework (5 minutes):** Students are to write a short account describing the events of 1917 after 16 March 1917, when Nicholas II abdicated. The points they should consider are on the task sheet.

**Make it easier!**
Try to make sure that everyone becomes involved. Encourage shy students to help make the presentations interesting and appealing. Lazier students should be watched and given specific areas to research.

**Make it harder!**
More able students could write a short passage on the Bolsheviks.

# Russia divided

In your group, decide where and what each of you will research to find out about one of the following:

1. Nicholas II
2. Rasputin
3. Alexander Kerensky
4. Vladimir Lenin
5. Leon Trotsky

You are to prepare a presentation about the person you have researched. With your group you will present to the rest of the class in the second half of the lesson. Your presentation should last up to 5 minutes and you must include:

- When and where the person was born.
- What he did.
- What he was like.
- At least one critical event that occurred in his life that affected history.

## Homework

Write a short account describing the events of 1917 after 16 March 1917, when Nicholas II abdicated. You should consider:

- What was the Provisional Government?
- Who returned to Russia in April 1917?
- Who or what were the Bolsheviks?
- What happened in October 1917?
- Did everyone agree with this?

# Rasputin (1)

**Introduction:** This will take two lessons. It introduces Rasputin and helps students to understand whether or not he added to the fall of the Romanov dynasty.

**Aims and outcomes:** At the end of the lesson, all students will recognize why Alexandra became enthralled with Rasputin and also why the Russian people did not sympathize with this. Most students will recognize the influence he had on the Tsarina and why this worried many Russians. Some students will be able to make informed judgements about his effect on the history of Russia.

**Starter (10 minutes):** Explain to the class that, in 1915, Tsar Nicholas went to the Front, taking over command of the Russian army from his uncle, the Grand Duke Nicholas. He left his wife, the Tsarina Alexandra, in charge of the government in St Petersburg, but she was extremely unpopular with the people. They mistrusted her because she was German so many thought that she must be a spy, but the main reason they disliked her was because of her relationship with Rasputin. Rasputin was a holy man, believed to have miraculous powers and Tsarina Alexandra – unknown to the public – believed he could cure her youngest son, Alexei, from an illness he was born with. There is an online sheet about Rasputin's life and death that you might like to use at this point.

Every student is to write a headline for an imaginary Russian newspaper in 1915. Give them 5 minutes to consider what it might say and ask them to share their headlines with the rest of the class after the time is up. Write some of the most interesting or eye-catching headlines on the board.

**Main phase (35 minutes):** During this lesson, students are to find out as much as they can about Rasputin and the people around him. They also need to understand the situation in Russia and Europe. This lesson is all about information gathering and the following lesson is about analysing and evaluating that information. If you can show any excerpts of films or documentaries on Rasputin, they will help students to remember facts, but there are also many books and websites. The film *Rasputin* from 1996 (directed by Udi Edel and written by Peter Pruce, with Alan Rickman in the title role) is worth showing if you can get a copy. Read the background information on Rasputin and display it on the board or hand out copies to the class.

**Plenary (10 minutes):** Ask the class who believes that Rasputin was a cause of the Russian Revolution? Give the class 10 minutes to discuss.

**Suggestion for homework (5 minutes):** Students are to write a timeline of Russian history from 1894 to 1916. As well as anything else they choose to include, they must also incorporate something about the following: Tsar Nicholas II; Tsarina Alexandra; Rasputin; Stolypin; the 1905 Revolution; World War I; Bloody Sunday.

**Make it easier!**

Less able students should be encouraged to write the names, Rasputin, Nicholas and Alexandra and list facts about them under their names.

**Make it harder!**

As well as making notes on those three, more able students should research Stolypin, Pavlovich and Yusupov.

# Rasputin (1)

You are to research all the main characters that you have heard about today, especially Rasputin, Nicholas II and Alexandra. You will need to make detailed notes, in preparation for writing the next lesson.

# 27 Rasputin (2) (over one or two lessons)

**Introduction:** Building on the previous lesson, this gives students the opportunity to delve deeper into the events and occurrences that they researched last lesson.

**Aims and outcomes:** At the end of the lesson, all students will be able to evaluate the different viewpoints of the Tsar and Tsarina, Rasputin and the Russian people. Most students will have a clear understanding of Rasputin's role in Russia's history and how far he contributed to the ruin of the monarchy. Some will be able to assess which of the stories about Rasputin were myths or facts.

**Starter (10 minutes):** As in the previous lesson, only this time informed by their research, ask students to write headlines for an imaginary Russian newspaper in 1915. After 5 minutes, ask them to share their headlines with the rest of the class. Write some of the most interesting or eye-catching headlines on the board and compare them to the headlines they wrote in the previous lesson. (If spreading this over two lessons, read out more during the second lesson's starter).

**Main phase for first lesson (40 minutes):** This continues from last lesson, underpinning the research students have already undertaken and developing their thoughts. Students are going to write diary entries (approximately half to one side of an A4 sheet) for two of the following people: Tsar Nicholas II, Tsarina Alexandra, Rasputin and a Russian. Read the task sheet and discuss with everyone the important features they need to research.

**Main phase for second lesson (40 minutes):** Students are to write diary entries (approximately half to one side of an A4 sheet) for the two people out of: Tsar Nicholas II, Tsarina Alexandra, Rasputin and a Russian that they did not write about in the previous half of this lesson. Read the task sheet and discuss with everyone the important features they need to research.

**Plenary for first lesson (5 minutes):** Discuss what students think in the light of their research. Who believes that Rasputin changed the course of Russian history? Who believes that he had a direct effect on the Russian Revolution? Ask who believes that he had little or no effect on it?

**Plenary for second lesson (10 minutes):** Students should volunteer their reasons for their beliefs as discussed in last lesson's plenary.

**Suggestion for homework (5 minutes):** Over two sessions of homework, students need to write an evaluation about Rasputin and whether or not he was a cause of the Russian Revolution. They should try to avoid concentrating too much on Rasputin's controversial life and death and try to focus on his impact on the government and society. Some students might need further things to consider:

- The poverty of the peasants and other problems facing Russia
- World War I
- Because the public did not know about Alexei's haemophilia, they were suspicious of Rasputin – if they had known, they might have been sympathetic
- Resentment of Alexandra – she was German and seemed aloof, but really she was preoccupied with her sick son
- Rasputin did damage the reputation of Nicholas and Alexandra, but did this cause the Russian Revolution?

(*continued over page 66*)

# Rasputin (2)

In the last lesson, you began to research prominent figures in this story. To evaluate whether or not Rasputin was a cause of the Russian Revolution, make sure your research is thorough enough. You are now going to write diary entries (approximately one side of an A4 sheet) for each of the following people:

- Tsar Nicholas II
- Tsarina Alexandra
- Rasputin
- A Russian

This is to help you understand each person's point of view and to evaluate the myth of Rasputin. So don't dwell too much on other incidents, but focus on the most important issues.

- For Nicholas II, consider how he felt – was he a family man; did he want to rule Russia? Did he think he was aligned to God? What was his life like? What was his opinion of a) Rasputin, b) his family and c) the Russian people?
- For Alexandra, consider her background and her priorities. What did she think of the Russian people; of her family and of Rasputin?
- For Rasputin, what do you believe was myth and what was the probable truth? What evidence can you find about the allegations spread about him? Was he a dangerous man or not?
- For 'a Russian' you can choose anyone – a peasant or worker if you like or a known character, such as Stolypin or Yusupov. If you choose an unknown, imagine what class that person is and remember their ignorance about Alexei's illness, so they will be suspicious of Rasputin. In addition, they will be aware of the unrest on the streets, of Bloody Sunday and of the assassinations of officials by workers.

In your diary entries, remember to write from your person's viewpoint, recount events in a logical order and include at times how the writer feels.

**Make it easier!**

Less able students could be helped with a template or outline for diary entries.

**Make it harder!**

More able students could be asked to come to the front of the class and read out their diary entries at the end of the lesson.

# 28 Russian rulers at the beginning of the 20th century

**Introduction:** This lesson will help students to understand the faults of the Tsar's government; what the Bolsheviks believed in and how and why they seized power in 1917.

**Aims and outcomes:** At the end of the lesson, all students will be able to describe some of the events that occurred in Russia from 1905 to 1918. Most students will be able to explain why the Bolsheviks were successful and some students will understand some of the most important reasons why they gained power.

**Starter (15 minutes):** Give students their task sheets and ask them to complete the missing word exercise in Part 1. The missing words are included in an online document, and you might like to display this after the exercise has been completed, or give it to less able students before you set the task.

**Main phase (35 minutes):** Give the class some background on the Russian calendar (available online) and then split the class into small groups. They should research and answer the questions in Part 2 of their task sheet. Within their small groups, students should discuss these points and carefully consider their answers.

**Plenary (10 minutes):** Explain that, by the turn of the twentieth century, Russian society was particularly divided and the Tsar was completely distanced from his people. Give the class some further information on why Tsar Nicholas II was not popular (there is some background information online). Ask the class why they think the Tsar was forced to abdicate in 1917? How important was World War I in this?

**Suggestion for homework (5 minutes):** Students are to write approximately 900 words, explaining why the Tsar was forced to abdicate in March 1917. They should also include whether or not World War I led to the collapse of the Russian monarchy (and if so, how much?).

**Make it easier!**
For the main part of the lesson, give more tips about what they should be considering and researching if you have students who find this difficult. Make sure in the plenary that everyone understands the issues and that this is a debate that is even now not resolved among historians.

**Make it harder!**
More able students might find the lesson starter quite straightforward, while less able students might struggle with it. At the end of the task, ask your ablest students to go over the answers and make sure that everyone understands the correct responses.

# Russian rulers at the beginning of the 20th century

## Part 1

At the turn of the twentieth century, ________________ lived in Russia, but only one per cent of these were ______________ and over 90 per cent were peasants, with the rest being middle class. Tsar Nicholas II ruled the whole of Russia, supported by the _________ church. Unrest among the poor grew – there were not enough jobs, their living conditions were awful and they were hungry, particularly as there had been a series of bad harvests. On top of everything else, Russia had performed poorly in a war against ______. In January 1905, a controversial Orthodox priest, George Gapon led 20,000 workers to the ______________ to deliver a petition to the Tsar. The Tsar was not in and his troops, not knowing what to do, fired at the crowd. More than 100 people were killed and the event became known as ______________. There was a strong reaction following this, with attacks on property and mutiny in the navy and unrest continued until 1914, when Russia entered ____________. Initially, people supported both the Tsar and the war, but Russian troops were poorly equipped and weak and ineffective leaders led them. Millions were killed and those that survived were starving. In 1915, the Tsar took control of the army, but of course, from then, he was blamed for every mistake. Strikes and mass demonstrations forced the Tsar to _________ in March 1917. Replacing Nicholas II was the ______________________ that was made up of members of several political parties – who found it difficult to agree on anything. The people wanted immediate changes, such as an end to the war, so the decision by the Provisional Government to continue was extremely __________. But other changes had taken place after the Tsar's abdication – one of these was the return to Russia of many of the revolutionary leaders. Most important among these was Lenin; the leader of the Bolsheviks.

## Part 2

Working in a small group, research and answer the following:

1. What is communism? Explain and give three points for and three points against it.
2. Who or what were the Bolsheviks? Explain and list three things that they did to ensure their power in Russia.
3. How did the Bolsheviks take power from the Provisional Government?
4. Why did they succeed?
5. How did the Bolsheviks try to create a more equal society in Russia?
6. In your opinion, were the Bolsheviks' actions necessary or unnecessary?

Discuss these points with your group and carefully consider your answers. Write in your exercise book or type and print on paper and stick that in your exercise book.

# 29 The Provisional Government and the Bolsheviks

**Introduction:** This lesson helps students to understand the failings of the Tsar's government, of the following Provisional Government and how and why the Bolsheviks came to power.

**Aims and outcomes:** At the end of the lesson, all students will understand why the Provisional Government failed and why the Bolsheviks took power. Most students will recognize that the situation in Russia called for a strong government and some students will understand how the new government gained control of Russia.

**Starter (10 minutes):** Everyone is to answer the multiple-choice questions on the task sheet. When they have finished, students are to swap their work with a partner and mark each other's answers.

**Main phase (35 minutes):** Discuss with the class why the situation in Russia encouraged the rise of socialist ideals. What was the Russian aristocracy like? What were the peasants' lives like? What is meant by socialist ideals? What can you tell others in the class about the Russian professional and industrial middle classes who wanted to be involved in decisions about their country? Do you know why factories were closing and food prices were soaring? What else was adding to discontent in the country?

Write their points on the board and then read out or display the background information that can be found online.

Working in pairs, students are to research the three issues on the task sheet and once they have done this, they are to write a short report on the reasons for the Bolsheviks' success in 1917.

**Plenary (10 minutes):** Give students a selection of sources about the Bolsheviks, such as quotations by Mikhail Uritsky, Anatoly Lunacharsky and Vladimir Lenin. Ask them to work in groups and discuss these, along with the information they have found during this lesson. Between them, they should analyse the Bolshevik Revolution in preparation for a written account for homework.

**Suggestion for homework (5 minutes):** Students should write an account explaining why the Provisional Government failed and why the Bolsheviks were successful.

**Make it easier!**
Make sure that less able students can understand the details they need to find for the main task of the lesson. If you think that some are not keeping up with the discussion, ask some of the class to explain it back or try drawing diagrams on the board to show them.

**Make it harder!**
More able students should write one short paragraph supporting the Bolsheviks and one short paragraph in opposition to them.

# The Provisional Government and the Bolsheviks

## Part 1

1. The Tsarist regime is also known as an
   a. Aristocracy
   b. Autocracy
   c. Orthodoxy
2. The Tsar's government printed money to pay for the war. This caused:
   a. Inflation
   b. Restoration
   c. Arbitration
3. When the Provisional Government took power, some of the most important issues it had to sort out immediately were:
   a. What to do about the war, jobs and food
   b. What to do about the shops, parks and roads
   c. Where to set up its headquarters
4. In 1917, the average worker's daily wage would buy:
   a. Three pieces of fruit and half a dozen eggs
   b. Less than half a bag of flour and just under a bag of potatoes
   c. Two pints of milk and a packet of biscuits
5. The Provisional Government failed to deal with the three great problems of:
   a. Sorting out the education system, building houses and lighting the roads
   b. Fighting World War I, giving land to the peasants and providing more food
   c. Creating more transport, ensuring everyone was warm and organizing the army

## Part 2

Working with a partner, research:

1. The Bolsheviks – who were they; what did they believe in; did people support them and why; how did they take power.
2. Lenin – why did he appeal to people; what were his personal qualities; his strengths as a leader.
3. The Mensheviks – who were they, what were their ideas based on, who led them?

Individually, now write a short report on the reasons for the Bolsheviks' success in 1917.

# 30 Murder of the monarchy

**Introduction:** Focusing on the execution of the Romanov family, this lesson examines why the Tsar and his family were all executed.

**Aims and outcomes:** At the end of the lesson, all students will understand why the Bolsheviks saw the Romanovs as a threat to their rule. Most students will recognize the mistakes that both the royal family and the Bolsheviks made and some students will be able to work out how the problems had been building up within the royal family and the Russian people for several generations.

**Starter (5–10 minutes):** Ask everyone why the Tsar and his family were a problem to the Communists? As the Tsar had abdicated in March 1917, why would the Bolsheviks have cared about him several months later? Explain that the Romanov dynasty had lasted 300 years, but Nicholas II was the last Tsar of Russia. After his abdication, the royal family was placed under house arrest. Why did the Bolsheviks do this?

**Main phase (35–40 minutes):** After you have explained or given students some resources to research further about the execution of the Romanov family, ask them to work individually to write and design a newspaper article. They need to know that various institutions supported the monarchy, including the Church, the nobility and some loyal peasants, while over half of the army and navy and many workers and the middle classes supported the Bolsheviks. For this task, students can choose from which viewpoint to take – that is, either for the Bolsheviks or for the Romanovs – but they must write as if the execution has not happened. In the article, they should include their opinion about the opposition, the situation in Russia at the time and the situation of the family – from either point of view.



**Plenary (10 minutes):** Put the class into two or three teams and ask them to write down the meanings of the following words (these are available online in case you'd like to display them on the board):

- Autocrat
- Cossacks
- Proletariat
- Bourgeois
- Revolutionaries

The first team to a) finish and b) use correct meanings should get a prize – which could be simply leaving the class first at the end of the lesson, or something else of your choice!

**Suggestion for homework (5 minutes):** Students should write a short passage explaining why they think that the murder of the Romanov family was either acceptable or unacceptable.

**Make it easier!**
You could try putting less able students with partners to write their articles.

**Make it harder!**
More able students could produce their articles on the computer, making them double page spreads.

# Murder of the monarchy

Using as many resources as you can, research further about the execution of the Romanov family. You are going to design and write a newspaper article. To prepare, you need to find out about the institutions that supported the monarchy, including the Church, the nobility and some loyal peasants, while over half of the army and navy and many workers and the middle classes supported the Bolsheviks. To the Bolsheviks, the family represented centuries of unfair government.

For this task, choose your viewpoint – that is, either for the Bolsheviks or for the Romanovs – but write as if the execution has not happened. In the article, include your opinion about the opposition, the situation in Russia at the time and the situation of the family – from either point of view.

Think how newspaper articles are written. You might want to give quotations from people or include pictures or a cartoon. Make your article as professional as you can.

# 31 How did the Bolsheviks rule?

**Introduction:** This lesson introduces students to the revolution from the Bolsheviks' point of view and gives them the opportunity to analyse the Bolsheviks' perspective and claims.

**Aims and outcomes:** At the end of the lesson, all students will understand the movements and approach of the Bolsheviks. Some of the questions in the lesson reiterate specific points and most students will recognize that certain aspects are crucial to understanding the lead-up to the Russian Revolution. Some students will gain greater understanding of Russian politics in 1917.

**Starter (15 minutes):** Recap with the class, by asking some questions at the start of the lesson. These are also available online in case you'd like to display them on the board:

1. Prior to 1917, where had Lenin been and why?
2. Why did the Germans support him?
3. When he returned, what made him successful?
4. What did the Bolsheviks promise the people?
5. Did everyone agree with the Bolsheviks? If not, why not?

They should write their answers in their work books and have a hands-up session to share their answers after 10 minutes. At this point, also make sure that they understand why the Provisional Government failed and why the Bolsheviks were able to take over in November 1917.

**Main phase (35 minutes):** Students are to research how Lenin and the Bolsheviks ruled Russia. You should give them some background information (there is a useful document online), and the task sheet gives some useful resources, but you should also provide other resources on the subject to give them a broad base from which to research. Once they have gathered sufficient information, they should answer the questions on the task sheet.



**Plenary (10 minutes):** Explain to the class that despite their claims, the majority of the Russian people did not support the Bolsheviks. They capitalized on the unpopularity of the Provisional Party and the fact that most of the army and navy supported them. There were approximately 800,000 members of the Bolshevik Party; they were disciplined and dedicated to revolution, but perhaps most importantly, they were the only party demanding that Russia should pull out of World War I. Make sure that everyone in the class is clear about the facts. If you have time, discuss the answers to the questions in the main part of the lesson.

**Suggestion for homework (5 minutes):** Students are to research Leon Trotsky. They should make notes on:

- His appeal or popularity – what made people like him?
- His personal qualities – for instance, was he kind, stern, warm or cold?
- His strengths as a leader – what did he do right, how did he give people confidence in his leadership?

**Make it easier!**

If some of your less able students are likely to struggle with the questions, put them into pairs or small groups, or help them individually to find relevant information in books or on websites.

**Make it harder!**

More able students could research and write a short piece on the communist laws that Lenin introduced.

# How did the Bolsheviks rule?

Research how Lenin and the Bolsheviks ruled Russia.

**Useful resources**

http://www.spartacus.schoolnet.co.uk/RUSbolsheviks.htm
http://www.marxists.org/subject/bolsheviks/index.htm
http://www.bbc.co.uk/schools/gcsebitesize/history/mwh/russia/leninandbolshevikrevolutionrev2.shtml

Once you have gathered sufficient information, answer the following:

1. Why was timing crucial to Lenin's success?
2. Who gave the Bolsheviks their arms and why?
3. Why were the Bolsheviks able to seize power in November 1917?
4. What were the three things that Lenin promised the Russian people when the Bolsheviks first came to power?
5. What did Lenin do to get Russia out of World War I?
6. What did the Bolsheviks do to all large businesses?
7. Who were the Cheka?
8. What did Lenin close in January 1918 and why?
9. What was the Bolshevik Party renamed in 1918?
10. Who opposed the Bolsheviks and what were they called?

# 32 Bolsheviks to communists

**Introduction:** This lesson considers the actions of the Communists, in particular, Lenin's actions.

**Aims and outcomes:** At the end of the lesson, all students will understand what the Communists were trying to do and why they gave up some of their territories. Most students will recognize that the Communists' actions were not as fair as they professed them to be and some students will be aware of the contrasting qualities of Lenin and Trotsky as indications of what was to happen later in Russia's history.

**Starter (10 minutes):** Ask the class to tell you about Trotsky, based on the research they undertook in a previous homework. Ask if anyone can tell you which two decrees Lenin took on taking power, (the Decree on Peace and the Decree on Land). Then give them some background information on the Decree of Peace (there is a document online that you can use).

**Main phase (35 minutes):** Students are asked on the task sheet to jot down quick answers to two points of view and to share their thoughts in a class discussion. Next, working in groups of three or four, they have 20 minutes to research the Communists, finding out:

- What did the Communists do to try to make Russia a more equal society?
- What did Lenin rename Russia in 1922 and what did this stand for?
- What happened to wealthy people?
- Do you think that the Communists were helping Russia to become a fairer society?

They should make notes together on these points and after 20 minutes, they should discuss their findings with the rest of the class.

**Plenary (10 minutes):** Remaining in their groups, ask students to plan a poster, imagining they are Russians in 1917, either for or against the Communists.

**Suggestion for homework (5 minutes):** Individually and in their own time, each student should create a poster, based on their ideas in the plenary. All posters should point out the main points of the students' propaganda.

**Make it easier!**
Less able students might need specific instructions about where to research the subject.

**Make it harder!**
More able students might have time to produce a poster showing one of the areas they have researched.

# Bolsheviks to communists

In rough, write down answers to the following and join in class discussion on the topics. Why was it:

a. important to sign the Treaty of Brest-Litovsk?

b. wrong to sign the Treaty of Brest-Litovsk?

Next, working in a small group, research the Communists to find answers to the following:

- What did the Communists do to try to make Russia a more equal society?
- What did Lenin rename Russia in 1922 and what did this stand for?
- What happened to wealthy people?
- Do you think that the Communists were helping Russia to become a fairer society?

Make notes together on these points and, after 20 minutes, you will be asked to discuss your groups' findings with the rest of the class.

# 33 Russian Civil War

**Introduction:** Examining the civil war that occurred after the Bolsheviks pulled out of the First World War, this lesson helps students to establish why the Russian Civil War occurred and its outcome.

**Aims and outcomes:** At the end of the lesson, all students understand the causes of the Russian Civil War and some of the differences between the opposing sides. Most students will understand how the Bolsheviks intimidated to keep control and some students will be aware of the plight of ordinary people during their regime.

**Starter (5–10 minutes):** In Part 1 on the task sheet, students are to fill in the gaps of the sentence completion exercise. The missing words are included in an online document. You could display them after the exercise has been completed, or give them to less able students before you set the task.

**Main phase (35–40 minutes):** In pairs or groups of three, students are to research the Russian Civil War, to find out the information listed on the task sheet and to write a piece for an imaginary news broadcast to present to the class as if they are television newsreaders.

**Plenary (10 minutes):** Students are to read out their 'news bulletins' to the rest of the class.

**Suggestion for homework (5 minutes):** Students are to answer the question: 'Why did the Bolsheviks win the Civil War?' They should consider the leadership of both Lenin and Trotsky, the locations of the Reds and the propaganda that they employed. Students can choose whether to write in full sentences or as bullet points.

**Make it easier!**

For the main task, try putting students in pairs or groups of mixed ability, or keep less able and more able students separate.

**Make it harder!**

If the school has the facilities, some more able students might be able to film their news broadcasts or, if not, simply act them out for the class.

# Russian Civil War

## Part 1

In 10 minutes, complete the following sentences

1. The Bolsheviks were known as the ____.
2. Lenin's activities made him unpopular, so in December 1917, he established the _____ (the secret police).
3. The Cheka launched a '___ ______' to terrorize the Bolsheviks' opponents, arresting and executing thousands – including the Tsar and his family.
4. Bolshevik opponents were made up mainly of royalists, middle-class industrialists and landowners and some loyal peasants. Although they were not united in their aims, they became known collectively as the ______.
5. Some of the Bolsheviks' opponents were former prisoners of war, known as the Czech Legion. In March 1918, they seized control of a large part of the _____________ _______.
6. Trotsky created the ___ ____ of over 300,000 men. He used fierce discipline to keep them under control and they were led by former Tsarist officers. Trotsky ensured their loyalty by holding their families hostage.

## Part 2

With a partner or a group of three, research the Russian Civil War. Find out the information listed below and write a piece for an imaginary news broadcast to present to the class as if you are a television newsreader. Information to find out:

- Why had the Bolsheviks become unpopular?
- What was the Constituent Assembly and what did the Bolsheviks do to it?
- The locations of the Reds and the Whites in Russia.
- What was War Communism?
- How did Trotsky discipline the Red Army?
- How did the civil war affect ordinary people?
- How did the Reds keep control and gain advantage?
- Why were the Whites disadvantaged?

# 34 The New Economic Policy (NEP)

**Introduction:** Considering the economic and political crisis in Russia, students will judge for themselves whether or not the NEP was a success.

**Aims and outcomes:** At the end of the lesson, all students will understand the reasons behind Lenin's New Economic Policy. Most students will recognize why this was not popular among many Bolsheviks and will also understand many of the reasons for the failure of the NEP. Some students will understand that the NEP restored the economy to pre-1914 levels, but that agricultural output increased faster than industrial output, which meant that peasants, even if they made money, could not spend it.

**Starter (10 minutes):** In pairs, give students 2 minutes to plan a discussion with the rest of the class about what they learned last time. Once every pair has had a turn, explain to the class that Lenin wanted socialism as described by Karl Marx (1818–83) the revolutionary German, credited as the founder of communism. Marx argued that for communism to work, everyone in the country must be at an even financial level. He said that capitalism produces internal tensions, which eventually lead to its destruction and that communism produces a stateless, classless society, which is the perfect situation. Central to Lenin's beliefs was the Marxist idea that capitalism and communism can never peacefully coexist and that historical forces would ultimately bring about the worldwide triumph of communism.

**Main phase (35 minutes):** The background information on the NEP in the task sheet is also available online, for easy display on the whiteboard. Everyone should read the task sheet then, in groups of four, students should research the NEP, listing its successes and failings. Next they should prepare questions on the topic and after 15 minutes, each group should ask another group their questions on the topic. You could make it into a quiz and give each team points. The winning team could be given a small reward of your choice.

**Plenary (10 minutes):** Ask one student if they think that the NEP allowed capitalism? If that student wishes to pass, ask them to ask the same question to someone else in the class and so on, 'passing it round' until someone answers correctly. Further questions to be asked and passed in this way are:

- Who led the Workers Opposition in 1921?
- Did the NEP restore prosperity to Russia?
- Why could the Communist Party not rely on free enterprise?
- Explain the 'Scissors Crisis'.

**Suggestion for homework (5 minutes):** Students should make an advertisement for an imaginary Russian newspaper of 1917, explaining the main points of the NEP.

**Make it easier!**

It is important that all students participate in the activities to gain understanding of the issues covered. Some students might try to avoid involvement, so you need to keep an eye on them and encourage contributions from all.

**Make it harder!**

More able students could prepare up to six relevant questions for the other group.

# The New Economic Policy (NEP)

After the Russian Civil War, the Russian economy was on the verge of collapse. So Lenin introduced the New Economic Policy (NEP). This was the opposite of War Communism and was designed to meet the urgent need for food. He issued a decree in March 1921, allowing peasants and farmers to give the government a specified amount of raw agricultural product as tax in kind. The state controlled banks, foreign trade and large industries (including coal, iron, steel and railways) but the Bolsheviks brought in experts on high wages, to increase production. The NEP allowed small businesses to make private profit and small factories were handed back to their owners. Where War Communism had forced peasants to hand over all surplus grain, Lenin let them sell any excess and pay a tax instead.

In a group of four, research the NEP using as many resources as you can, listing its successes and failings. Next, prepare three questions on the topic. After 20 minutes, you will ask one of the other groups your three questions.

# 35 Trotsky and Stalin

**Introduction:** This lesson examines the political situation in Russia after Lenin's death in 1924.

**Aims and outcomes:** At the end of the lesson, all students will recognize the qualities that made both Trotsky and Stalin candidates to lead the Communist Party. Most students will recognize Trotsky's false sense of security was part of his downfall and some students will realize that as well as chance events, Stalin had foresight and cunning, which helped to secure his power, even though this took five years.

**Starter (15 minutes):** Recap with the class that in January 1924, Lenin died (there is a useful online resource for this). They can confer quietly with each other for this first part of the lesson. Their task is to create timelines of Russia from the period 1917 to 1924. They should include something about the following:

- World War I
- The October Revolution
- The New Economic Policy
- Abdication of the Tsar
- The Treaty of Brest-Litovsk
- The Russian Civil War
- War Communism
- Trotsky's Red Army
- The Provisional Government



Plus anything else they feel to be important.

**Main phase (35 minutes):** Everyone should read the task sheet carefully and then follow the instructions in Part 2. They are to work individually, dividing two pages into two separate columns. On one page, they should list Trotsky's and Stalin's attributes for leadership of the Communist Party, and on the other page they should list Trotsky and Stalin's respective weaknesses. Finally, they are to make a poster or advertisement, campaigning for either Trotsky or Stalin to head the Communist Party, announcing their chosen candidate's qualities.

**Plenary (5 minutes):** Students should take it in turns to show their posters or advertisements to the rest of the class and everyone should critique them – being as positive as possible, about what works well.

**Suggestion for homework (5 minutes):** Why did Stalin win? Students should summarize the reasons for Stalin's success in heading the Communist Party. They should consider not only the two men's personalities and attitudes but also what they thought of each other, what the people who knew them thought of them, key events in their lives and a conclusion.

**Make it easier!**
Some students might need further guidance from you. It is also important that everyone understands why Stalin and not Trotsky eventually emerged as Lenin's successor, so less able students might benefit if you stop the lesson occasionally to ask individuals to give information on their research in progress.

**Make it harder!**
More able students should write a short passage or numbered points about why Stalin and not Trotsky took power after Lenin's death.

# Trotsky and Stalin

## Part 1

The Russian Civil War had cost even more Russian lives than in World War I and before the NEP; the Russian economy was in ruins. In 1918, Lenin was shot twice by a Socialist revolutionary. He was not killed, but in 1922 he suffered a stroke and then three more in 1923. The strokes left him severely disabled and in January 1924, he died. There were several Communist figures who were possible candidates to take his place but instead of holding elections, the Communist Party chose the person who showed the greatest power within the party. Among the contenders were two men who became bitter rivals. They were Leon Trotsky and Joseph Stalin.

## Part 2

Divide a page in your exercise book or a sheet of paper into two columns. In one column, list Trotsky's qualities for leadership of the Communist Party, and in the other column, list Stalin's qualities for leadership of the Communist Party. Next, divide another page in the same way, only this time list Trotsky and Stalin's individual weaknesses. Finally, make a poster or advertisement on paper, campaigning for either Trotsky or Stalin to head the Communist Party, announcing your chosen candidate's qualities.

**Useful links**

http://www.fbuch.com/leon.htm
http://www.bbc.co.uk/history/historic_figures/trotsky_leon.shtml
http://www.bbc.co.uk/history/historic_figures/stalin_joseph.shtml
http://www.spartacus.schoolnet.co.uk/RUSstalin.htm

# Stalin and the creation of the USSR

**Introduction:** This lesson expands on the previous one – or on any introduction to Stalin, with students undertaking research into his dictatorship.

**Aims and outcomes:** At the end of the lesson, all students will be aware of Stalin's Five-Year Plans and the way that he intimidated the Russian people. Most students will recognize the successes and failures of Stalin's industrializations and some students will recognize that the problems included poor quality housing; long working hours and low pay and that unethical labour camps provided much of the workforce.

**Starter (10 minutes):** To recap on previous learning, give students some questions (also available online) to answer at the beginning of the lesson:

1. Where was Joseph Stalin born?
2. What did the name Stalin mean?
3. How many times was Stalin exiled and arrested?
4. What worried people about Trotsky's ideas?
5. Why did Trotsky not attend Lenin's funeral?
6. What happened to Trotsky in 1929?

**Main phase (40 minutes):** Go through Stalin's Five-Year Plans with the class (you might want to refer to the online summary for this). Next, divide the class into four teams (easy-to-cut cards are also available online). Give each team one aspect of Stalin's rule to research as follows:

*Team 1: Gulag*
Find out about the conditions of the labour camps and prisons; who was put into them; why they were put there; how many people were possibly put in them during Stalin's rule; what they had to do as punishments and what their living conditions were like.

*Team 2: Collectivization*
Find out: what it was; why it was introduced; what happened to the farmers and what happened to those who did not cooperate.

*Team 3: Stakhanovites*
Find out where the name came from; what it meant; how Russians responded and what they were rewarded with if they succeeded. Why did Stalin reward them?

*Team 4: Terror*
Find out how Stalin kept control; what he did to his opponents; his secret police; how he convicted and punished people; what was it like living under Stalin's rule?

After 15 minutes, bring the class back to present their findings to each other. Everyone should make notes. Once the research has been shared, ask the class: Why did Stalin industrialize the USSR? Using the points on their sheets, they should assess them with the understanding they have gained this lesson and write them down in order of importance.

**Plenary (5 minutes):** Ask the class the following questions, inviting students to put up their hands if they know the answer.

(*continued over page 86*)

# Stalin and the creation of the USSR

**Your task:** You are going to be put into one of four teams in the class. You have 15 minutes to research and make notes. Discuss your findings with the class and decide: Why did Stalin industrialize the USSR? Which of the following points do you think are the most important? Write them down in order of importance:

- To make the USSR strong
- To make goods to export
- For Stalin to achieve recognition as a great statesman
- To give ordinary Russians a better standard of living
- To show that communism works
- To help the country recover from wars and revolutions
- To crush Stalin's opponents
- To make the USSR independent from other countries

1. What good came out of Stalin's Five-Year Plans?
2. In what year was his first Five-Year Plan?
3. What might the peasants have found difficult?
4. How much of the USSR was collectivized?
5. Which do you think was more successful: collectivization or industrialization?
6. Was Gulag necessary? Why did Stalin do this?

**Suggestion for homework (5 minutes):** Everyone is to write two lists, describing the failures and successes of Stalin's industrialization of the USSR. They should consider all the work they have done in class and also conduct further individual research. If your students need extra guidance, you can give them this information:

- The USSR needed to catch up with other industrialized countries
- Stalin implemented some of Trotsky's ideas to modernize the USSR
- The Five-Year Plans set targets for everyone to aim for; so everyone knew what they had to do
- Many of the targets were too high, but they were to raise the USSR's achievements
- The first Five-Year Plan (1928–33) focused on coal, steel, railways and other heavy industries
- The second Five-Year Plan (1932–37) focused on weapons and protection as Hitler rose in power in Germany
- In less than ten years, the USSR's industrial output almost doubled – but ordinary people had miserable lives as a result

**Make it easier!**

If your students learn more with visual stimulus, show them this website on Gulag:

http://www.osa.ceu.hu/gulag/index.html

More able students might find the following website useful:

http://chnm.gmu.edu/wwh/modules/lesson11/lesson11.php?s=0

The following web resources should be useful for all abilities:

http://www.learningcurve.gov.uk/heroesvillains/g4/cs2/default.htm

**Make it harder!**

More able students could work in pairs and write a short 'interview with Stalin' entitled 'Man of Steel'.

# Section E Germany

# 37 Weaknesses of the Weimar Republic

**Introduction:** This lesson considers the flaws of the Weimar Republic; its constitution and weaknesses within the system.

**Aims and outcomes:** At the end of the lesson, all students will understand the weaknesses of the Weimar Republic. Most students will recognize that the attitude of the German people affected the Republic's successes and failures. Some students will understand that the downfall of the Weimar Republic arose through a complex series of events and decisions.

**Starter (10–15 minutes):** Introduce the Weimar Constitution. Explain how it was structured, then give the class the following titles with snippets of information. Draw a plan of the Weimar Constitution as it was structured on the board:

- The German people – all adults could vote
- The Chancellor – appointed from the Reichstag by the President
- The Reichstag – proportional representation; parties had the same proportion of seats as their proportion of votes
- The President – elected every seven years

**Main phase (35–40 minutes):** Introduce students to the weaknesses of the system (there is an internet resource on the Weimar Republic's problems). Mention, for instance, the enemies of the Republic, proportional representation, the President having too much power, and the Chancellor being elected by the President. They should read the task sheet carefully and follow instructions about researching and making thorough notes in their exercise books.

**Plenary (5–10 minutes):** After ascertaining what they have found out during the main part of the lesson, recap with the class about Germany's problems under the Weimar Republic (bullet points also available online):

- Throughout the Weimar Republic no single party ever won a majority of seats in the Reichstag (German parliament)
- In 1925 Hindenburg was elected president – he was a prominent critic of the Weimar Republic
- The Weimar Republic became too dependent on American loans
- There were extremes of wealth (rich industrialists) and poverty (high unemployment)

Online there is also a useful summary of the threats to the Weimar Republic that are referred to in the task sheet.

**Suggestion for homework (5 minutes):** Explain to the class that 1923 later became known as 'the year of crises'. For homework, they are to research and write in bullet points, the main events or actions of Gustav Stresemann, from 1923 to 1929. They should call their work 'The Stresemann Years' and it should take two parts:

1. As Chancellor (1923–24)
2. As Foreign Minister (1924–29)

Outline details are on the task sheet.

(*continued over page 90*)

# Weaknesses of the Weimar Republic

You should call your work 'The Stresemann Years' and it should take two parts:

1. As Chancellor (1923–24) – no longer able to pay the striking workers, more money was printed, which finally led to hyperinflation. Stresemann ended this disastrous process by introducing a new currency, the Rentenmark, which reassured the people that the democratic system was willing and able to solve urgent problems. He stopped passive resistance in the Ruhr. The government (under his rule) was strongly right wing and he gave orders that the left-wing state governments in Saxony and Thuringia should be deposed. In 1924, Germany agreed to resume reparation payments and accepted a huge loan from the Allies.
2. As Foreign Minister (1924–29) – in 1925, Germany signed the Locarno Treaties with Britain, France and Italy. This guaranteed Germany's frontiers with France and Belgium. In 1926, Stresemann took Germany into the League of Nations, which meant that Germany would have a recognized seat next to Britain and France. In 1929, the Young Plan produced a final agreement on reparations – also the Allies must leave the Rhineland.

Your task is to research threats to the Weimar Republic, including:

1. Kapp Putsch
2. The Occupation of the Ruhr
3. Inflation
4. The Munich Putsch

As you research, use those headings and write down your findings in your exercise book.

**Make it easier!**

If the pace of the lesson is too fast for some students, you could extend this lesson to take two sessions, or help some of the slower workers with further guidance for the research, or put them with a partner who can help.

**Make it harder!**

More able students should find out what were the two main flaws of the Weimar Republic and why do they think that those two were the main ones?

# TIPS: Weaknesses of the Weimar Republic Topic Tips

- Make sure that your students realise that causes are always linked to ideas, attitudes and beliefs of the particular time, so they should try to imagine what it was like to live in Weimar at that time and find as many sources as possible that clarify this.
- They should always try to find factual examples, references or sources and consider the problem from several different perspectives.
- By now all your students should be able to use sources analytically to reach logical and validated conclusions. If they are still struggling, introduce a lesson on sources as a refresher or revision course.
- Introduce students to all Germany's political parties between 1919 and 1923. They should find out which parties supported the Republic and which were against it?
- Everyone should be clear about the meanings of hyperinflation and proportional representation.
- All students should be clear that the Kaiser was effectively a dictator and in contrast, the Weimar Constitution tried to set up the most democratic system in the world, where no one could become too powerful, with a system of proportional representation. Right and left-wing extremism was also responsible for the volatility of the Weimar Republic. They should be aware of strikes and demonstrations and the Kapp Putsch and Munich Putsch.

# The Nazi Party (over one or two lessons)

**Introduction:** This lesson introduces students to the main aims and goals of the Nazi Party.

**Aims and outcomes:** At the end of the lesson, all students will understand some of the tactics that the Nazi Party took when they were aiming for power. Most students will recognize that their intentions were to bring Germany back to greatness and some students will realize that external issues and events added to their rise to power.

**Starter for first lesson (15 minutes):** Show the class a picture of the Nazi swastika (available online) and ask them to say what they think it is. Does it mean anything to anyone? Do they recognize it? If possible, show them the swastika in different colours and ask them to describe the kind of image each colour combination portrays. In the same online document there is information about the symbolism of the swastika: this can be displayed, read to the class or printed off and given out to some or all students. Can there be two completely opposite meanings for one symbol? Discuss.

**Main phase for first lesson (35 minutes):** Ask the class what they think the Nazi Party believed in. Put them in groups of between four and six and give them 15 minutes to research this. After the 15 minutes, discuss with them what the Nazi Party believed in. Information and pointers are on the task sheet. Ask everyone why they were called the National Socialist Party and discuss. (They should realize that although the party seemed right wing, members actually wanted votes from both left- and right-wing supporters).

**Main phase for second lesson (45 minutes):** As in Part 3 on their task sheets, back in their groups from the last lesson, students are to research the rise of the Nazi Party. They are to look into the Munich Putsch, Hitler's spell in prison and what he did there, his charisma and powers as an orator, the 1924 Reichstag elections and following election of 1928, the weaknesses of the Weimar Government and the rise of extremism and increase of political violence. After they have researched these topics, each group is to produce a poster on A3 or A2 paper for the Nazi Party in the mid-1920s. They should decide who they are aiming at, such as women, the general public, workers or families and so on.

**Plenary for first lesson (10 minutes):** Discuss what symbolic significance Hitler had for choosing the swastika and the colours of the Nazi flag, why Hitler discarded the traditional flag in favour of the Nazi flag and whether they think that the swastika should be banned from public display today.

**Plenary for second lesson (10 minutes):** Groups are to present their posters. The rest of the class should be able to ask questions about them and each group to respond to the questions, explaining why they chose the images and words and who they were aiming to reach. If possible, show them a selection of posters from Germany at the time. There are some excellent images on this site:

http://www.bbc.co.uk/history/worldwars/wwtwo/nazi_propaganda_gallery.shtml

**Suggestion for homework (5 minutes):** Students are to write a passage of at least 400 words, explaining why the Nazis put so much effort into propaganda.

(*continued over page 94*)

# The Nazi Party

## Part 1

What do you think the Nazi Party believed in? In the group you have been put in, you have 5 minutes to research this. At the end of 5 minutes, join in class discussion about what the Nazi Party believed in. In your research, include:

- Abolish the Treaty of Versailles
- Destroy the Weimar Republic
- Destroy Marxism
- Remove Jews from all positions of leadership in Germany
- No non-Germans could be newspaper editors
- Educate gifted children at the State's expense
- Increase old age pensions
- Have a strong central government
- Challenge terror with their own terror or violence
- Nationalize important industries
- Re-arm German troops
- Re-establish the Freikorps as the SA (Storm troopers) to protect Nazi speakers from left-wing opponents

Why were they called the National Socialist Party? (Although the party seemed right wing, members actually wanted votes from both left- and right-wing supporters).

## Part 2

Next, remaining in your group, research the rise of the Nazi Party. Look into the Munich Putsch, Hitler's spell in prison and what he did there, his charisma and powers as an orator, the 1924 Reichstag elections and following election of 1928, the weaknesses of the Weimar Government and the rise of extremism and increase of political violence. After you have researched, work with your group to produce a poster on A3 or A2 paper for the Nazi Party in the mid-1920s. Decide who you are aiming at, such as women, the general public, workers or families and so on.

**Make it easier!**
Try to gauge which groups are producing the best posters and ask those groups to show their work first. Mixing abilities within each group works with some students or you might find that you can mix creative and analytical minds within the groups to good effect.

**Make it harder!**
More able students will be able to ascertain why Hitler appealed to German people at that time – and the types of people he appealed to most. They could write a short passage on this in their exercise books.

# TIPS: The Nazi Party Topic Tips

- Students should be aware of how Hitler took absolute control over the Nazi Party, asserting the Leadership Principle; restructuring the party; using propaganda to focus on particular complaints and used the Nazi Party's newspaper, the *Völkischer Beobachter*, to broaden his plans; he emphasised national pride with a sense of belonging and loyalty and among other things, he promised to destroy the Versailles Treaty.
- Students should be introduced into some of the ways in which democracy was failing even before Hitler manipulated events.
- It will be helpful if they understand that Hitler controlled the mass media, using modern and effective methods, promising a lot, but saying little, not explaining their policies so that they could not be criticised and banning meetings of the Opposition.
- Students need to understand the importance of propaganda in Nazi Germany, how it was controlled and why it was so important to the Nazis. As Goebbels said: "The essence of propaganda consists in winning people over to an idea so sincerely, so vitally, that in the end they succumb to it utterly and can never escape from it."

# 39 How Hitler took control

**Introduction:** This lesson helps students to consider how Hitler took control of Germany. Students will be able to evaluate for themselves, the most important events and factors, which helped him to dictatorship.

**Aims and outcomes:** At the end of the lesson, all students will recognize how Hitler capitalized on the despair in Germany following World War I and the Treaty of Versailles. Most students will recognize how he became a dictator and of many of the legitimate and underhand methods he used to gain control. Some students will be aware of the widespread influence he developed and how he used both intimidating and psychological methods to inspire and persuade.

**Starter (15 minutes):** Show the class some images from the Nuremberg Rallies, such as:

http://www.leninimports.com/nuremberg_party_rallies.html
http://americanpicturelinks.com/Images/1936NurembergRally%5B1%5D.jpg
http://www.earthstation1.com/WWIIPics/Germany/Hitler/HitlerAddressesRallyAtDortmund1933.jpg

These links are also available directly from the website.

Explain that for one week each September, from 1923 to 1938, thousands of German people travelled to the city of Nuremberg for the annual rally of the Nazi Party. People packed into a huge stadium to watch rows of soldiers march, to hear bands play and to listen to the leader of the Nazi Party, Adolf Hitler, as he talked and inspired them all. Discuss with the class: Where did Hitler come from? How did he become the leader of the Nazi Party? How do the pictures show Hitler's power? Why did so many people want to hear him speak? What did he speak about? How were German people feeling at the time?

**Main phase (35 minutes):** Students are going to work out for themselves why Hitler became Chancellor in 1933. You should talk them through the facts about Hitler in the online document, then they will research the main methods Hitler used to become Chancellor. They should use whatever resources available to them and investigate the points in Part 2 on the task sheet

**Plenary (5 minutes):** Discuss what everyone has found out. Ask students to think about what they consider to be the most important reasons that Hitler became Chancellor and help them to plan how they might write about this.

**Suggestion for homework (5 minutes):** Using their research and planning, students should write a piece of about 500–600 words entitled 'Why did Hitler become Chancellor in 1933?'

**Make it easier!**
If less able students do not find out enough information, point out to them further information that they should understand and use a subsequent lesson to help them to understand more details.

**Make it harder!**
More able students should be able to gather plenty of relevant information during the lesson and should be able to plan and write an intelligent and clearly thought-out piece.

# How Hitler took control

## Part 1

Why did Hitler become Chancellor in 1933?

## Part 2

Research the main methods Hitler used to become Chancellor. Use whatever resources are available and investigate:

- The weakness of the Weimar Republic (specifically, unpopular economic policies, such as increasing taxes, cutting wages and decreasing unemployment benefits)
- Hitler's reorganization of the Nazi Party after his release from prison
- Gaining the support of the working classes and increasing the anti-Jewish propaganda
- The publication of *Mein Kampf*
- Training members of the Nazi Party in public speaking
- The ability and willingness to change their policies to meet what people found interesting
- Propaganda and public speaking
- Giving hope to the depressed German public
- General von Schleicher

# 40 How did Hitler consolidate his power?

**Introduction:** This lesson helps students to understand how Hitler established and strengthened his power in Germany.

**Aims and outcomes:** At the end of the lesson, all students will understand the power that Hitler gained through foresight and intimidation. Most students will recognize that a series of events and coincidences also added to Hitler's supremacy and some students will conclude that certain unexplained events were also the responsibility of the Nazi Party in order to gain greater popularity.

**Starter (15 minutes):** If possible, show everyone some sources about the SS (Shutzstaffel), the Gestapo and concentration camps; explain how people, such as Jews and Communists, were imprisoned without trial. See who remembers what anti-Semitism means and discuss how else Hitler controlled the people. Recap about Joseph Goebbels' role as Minister of Propaganda and consider Hitler's rallies and control of publications in Germany. Next, review what your students know about the Hitler Youth and how Hitler trained and controlled children and young people growing up in Germany during the 1930s. Encourage everyone to participate in this discussion. Finally, talk to them about the economic depression and how Hitler overcame this in Germany and how he created jobs.

**Main phase (30 minutes):** After a fairly in-depth lesson starter, give students the task sheets and ask them to answer the ten questions. They should answer each question with at least three sentences.

**Plenary (10 minutes):** Ask the class to create a timeline of Hitler's road to dictatorship. You could allow students to take it in turns to write years and events on the board, with everyone writing this down in their books. As students write on the board, others should either agree or disagree, so the timeline will be completed to everyone's approval. You could give them the first event that they could begin with 30 January 1933 with Hitler becoming Chancellor and the last event as 2 August 1934 with Hitler becoming the Führer and Reich Chancellor after Hindenburg died and the army swearing an oath to him.

**Suggestion for homework (5 minutes):** Students are to write a passage of at least 500 words, describing the structure of the Nazi Party. They should begin with Hitler as leader, giving orders and receiving information from 42 district leaders who gave orders to area leaders, then local group leaders and so on. Give extra marks for those who include the block leaders and their power to put their neighbours into concentration camps.

**Make it easier!**
Notice any students trying to avoid participation. It often helps to stop students during an activity and ask who has found out any particularly interesting or relevant information and to make sure that everyone includes some key facts.

**Make it harder!**
More able students could research the organization of the Nazi Party and in a small group, could present their findings to the rest of the class.

# How did Hitler consolidate his power?

Writing in your exercise book and using all resources you can, answer each question below with at least three sentences:

1. When he first became Chancellor, what did Hitler persuade President Hindenburg to do?
2. Why was the Reichstag fire important?
3. Who do you think started the fire?
4. Was Hitler pleased or disappointed with the results of the election on 5 March 1933? Why was this?
5. Explain how Hitler managed to secure more power in March 1933, despite the results of the election?
6. What happened on the 'Night of the Long Knives'?
7. Why did Hitler order the SS to execute so many members of the SA?
8. What did Hitler do to Trade Unions?
9. What was the Concordat?
10. What was the *Enabling Act*?

# 41 The Police State and opposition to the Nazis

**Introduction:** This lesson helps students to understand the amount of policing that the Nazi Party introduced and also the opposition to the Nazis within Germany.

**Aims and outcomes:** At the end of the lesson, all students will understand what forms of intimidation the Nazis used to gain and retain power during the 1930s. Most students will recognize that if there was opposition, most German people were scared to voice any opposition and that propaganda concealed any underhand activities from them anyway. Some students will be aware of the passive resistance and non-cooperation that became quite common during the mid to late 1930s.

**Starter (15 minutes):** Put students into six groups and ask them to research the following about Germany during the 1930s:

Group 1: The SS
Group 2: Concentration camps
Group 3: The Gestapo
Group 4: Police, courts and prisons
Group 5: Informers
Group 6: Heinrich Himmler

Students should only be given a few minutes to research their topics and then they should present their findings to the class. They may choose spokespeople from within their groups or all take part in the presentation. As it is only a quick investigation and presentation, they should only have time to find out and present the main points. Everyone should make notes on all the topics researched and presented.

**Main phase (30 minutes):** Remaining in their groups, if possible, show the whole class some images of Nazi propaganda posters. This is a useful site:

http://www.calvin.edu/academic/cas/gpa/posters2.htm

Ask each group to select three of the posters and, within their groups, discuss the questions on Part 1 of the task sheet. Then they should make notes and after about 15 minutes, each group should explain about one poster of their choice, using their research. Finally they should write a paragraph to answer Part 2 on the task sheet.

**Plenary (10 minutes):** On the board, write a list of some of the forms opposition to a political party might take, such as: Attempted coups d'etat; underground resistance; open opposition; passive resistance and non-cooperation or private grumbling. For each, explain, or ask the students to explain the meanings. Taking each of these methods of opposition, one-by-one, ask the class if they believe that any of these took place in Germany when the Nazis were first in power. They must explain why they believe their answers.

**Suggestion for homework (5 minutes):** Students are to research any opposition to the Nazi Party within Germany in the mid to late 1930s and if so, what forms this opposition took.

*(continued over page 102)*

# The Police State and opposition to the Nazis

## Part 1

After you have looked at images of Nazi propaganda posters, within your group, select three of the posters and decide between you the following questions about each one:

a. What can I learn from this source?

b. What is being said or shown?

c. When was it produced?

d. Where was it produced?

e. Why did the Nazis produce it?

f. What evidence do we have to support these points?

Make notes and after about 15 minutes, you are going to explain about one poster of your choice, using your answers to the above questions and your conclusions.

## Part 2

Do you think that the German people were afraid of the Nazis, or do you think that they believed that the Nazis would help them? Was there any opposition to Nazi rule? Write down a paragraph explaining your thoughts on this.

**Make it easier!**

If necessary, put groups of less motivated students together and keep questioning them and making sure that they are participating properly.

**Make it harder!**

More able students should write a short passage in their exercise books explaining how Hitler changed Germany from a democracy to a dictatorship.

# TIPS: The Police State and Opposition to the Nazis Topic Tips

Here are further useful resources:

http://www.bbc.co.uk/schools/gcsebitesize/history/mwh/germany/oppositionrev1.shtml
http://remember.org/guide/Facts.root.nazi.html
http://www.ushmm.org/wlc/en/article.php?ModuleId=10005208
http://www.bbc.co.uk/learningzone/clips/opposition-to-the-war-in-germany/3265.html
http://www.bbc.co.uk/schools/gcsebitesize/history/mwh/germany/controlstructurerev_print.shtml

- Students should be aware that most Germans were supportive of Hitler as he was seen to be reducing unemployment. Active resistance against the Nazis occurred with less than 1% of the German population. There was a low level of resistance for many reasons, including the authoritarian nature of the Nazi rule; the fear that people would lose their jobs; greater fear of imprisonment or even death; so many Germany were forced into accepting the regime whether they liked it or not.
- Students should be aware of where the SS came from – about 55% were unemployed, many were ex-servicemen from World War I and they were all devoted to Hitler personally. They were disciplined and well-ordered and they gave many Germans reassurance. The SS grew into a huge organization with many different responsibilities. The main responsibility, however, was to destroy any opposition to the Nazis. Two sub-divisions of the SS were: Death's Head Units, which were responsible for concentration camps and killing Jews, and the Waffen-SS, which were armoured sections that fought beside the regular army.

# 42 How did the Nazis deal with the churches?

**Introduction:** Beginning with a review about past topics, this lesson continues with the topic of who opposed the Nazis in Germany.

**Aims and outcomes:** At the end of the lesson, all students will understand why Christian church leaders in Germany opposed the Nazis. Most students will be aware of the methods that Hitler used to subdue the Christian churches in Germany and some students will recognize some of the main German church leaders and what they opposed in particular about the Nazi Party and how they were treated.

**Starter (10 minutes):** For a quick recap on previous lessons, ask students to write down one sentence to explain the meanings of the following words:

- Armistice
- Communism
- Democracy
- Dictator
- Nazis
- Propaganda
- Revolution
- Suffragettes
- Treaty

The list of words to define is also available online: you might like to display it on the board.

**Main phase (35 minutes):** Read the online summary of the Church in Nazi Germany and instruct everyone to follow the instructions in Part 1 to make a chart with four vertical columns.

**Plenary (10 minutes):** Instruct everyone to read Part 2 on the task sheet and to fill in the missing words. The missing words are included on an online document, and you might like to display this after the exercise has been completed, or give it to less able students before you set the task.

**Suggestion for homework (5 minutes):** Students should write a passage answering the question: 'How effectively did the Nazis deal with their opponents during the mid-1930s?'

**Make it easier!**

For Part 1 of the task sheet, less able students might be better in a group of four; they can produce their own charts, but help each other as they work.

**Make it harder!**

More able students that are speeding ahead with their work, can be given some extension work, such as working out through research, what changed in Hitler's regime/the Nazi Party in the 1930s from its beginnings in the 1920s.

# How did the Nazis deal with the churches?

## Part 1

Make a chart with four vertical columns. Horizontally, list the main leaders of churches in Germany when the Nazis came to power. Research these leaders (such as Paul Schneider, Josef Fath or Cardinal Galen) and also add Jehovah's Witnesses or any other Christian religion that opposed the Nazis. In the first column, write the names of these people, in the second column, write which branch of Christianity they followed: Catholic, Protestant, Jehovah's Witness and so on. In the third column, write 'What did they oppose?' In the final column, write 'How were they dealt with?'

## Part 2

The _______ in Nazi Germany was seen by Hitler as a threat that should not be tolerated. The Catholic Church wanted __________ to spread across Germany from Russia, but the Nazis held had viewed the Nazis as a barrier to the spread of communism from Russia. In 1933, Hitler and the Catholic Church signed an agreement known as a __________ that he would not interfere with the Catholic Church and the Church would not comment on politics. Nevertheless, in 1937 Hitler began arresting priests from the _________ Church. In 1937, the Pope, Pius XI, issued a statement proclaiming his anxiety over what was happening in Germany. The ___________ Church was made up of a collection of several churches, which made them easier to deal with than the Catholics.

In 1936, the Nazis created the Reich Church, using a _________ rather than a cross as its symbol. Ludwig Muller, who had been given the title of 'Reich Bishop' by Hitler in 1933, led the 'German Christians'. Muller and the Reich Church believed that any member of the church who had ______ ancestry should be turned away.

Anyone who opposed Hitler and the Reich Church was arrested by the Gestapo and sent to a ______________ camp. The _____ was replaced by *Mein Kampf* on the altar, with a sword next to it.

# 43 What was the Nazis' approach to young people in Germany?

**Introduction:** This lesson helps students to understand the fulfilment of Hitler's aim to control every aspect of life in Germany, especially young and influential minds.

**Aims and outcomes:** At the end of the lesson, all students will recognize some ways that the Nazis shaped young minds. Most will be aware of the extent of the Nazis indoctrination and how they used both force and persuasion to influence people growing up in Germany. Some will understand how many young people believed that Hitler was leading them to a brighter future.

**Starter (10 minutes):** Ask students why they think that Hitler focused on German children and teenagers? Explain that he wanted to make them all good Nazis, with the same beliefs, aims and hopes. He controlled schools and how children and young people spent their spare time. He encouraged boys to want to fight for their country and girls to focus on 'children, church and kitchen' or 'kinder, kirche und küche'. They were all taught Nazi policies and beliefs. Ask students to quickly jot down why they think the Hitler youth was popular. Give them a couple of minutes to write down as many reasons as they can. These could include: it gave them something to do; they were treated as if they were special; they were given their own uniform, which gave them a feeling of belonging; they felt patriotic and part of a big and special country/organization; it made them feel as if they were the future, so had a vital role in Germany's expectations.

**Main phase (35 minutes):** In pairs, students are to research education in Nazi Germany, to find out as much as they can about the way the education system was structured, what boys learned, what girls learned and how teachers were trained and treated. As explained in Part 1, they should write a column for an imaginary German newspaper of the mid-1930s.

**Plenary (10 minutes):** Ask everyone to read Part 2 of the task sheet. As they study the timetable, ask students why they think that German was taught so much – see who can tell you it taught students to be conscious of their national identity by learning and reading about German heroes and strengths. Find out if they understand that in Geography and History, students learned about the land that Germany used to own and how Germany used to be powerful and successful, and why they think that there was so much exercise and sport. Do they know what 'Eugenics' was about? (It was the study of, or belief in, the possibilities of improving the qualities of the human race by stopping people with genetic defects or undesirable traits from reproducing).

**Suggestion for homework (5 minutes):** Students are to research whether all young people supported the Nazis. They could research groups such as the 'Swing' movement or the Edelweiss Pirates. Give them those two names and ask them to make notes on what they discover – that is, what these movements were, who belonged to them, what they believed and how they were treated by the Nazis.

**Make it easier!**

Some students might need to be encouraged to participate and everyone should be encouraged to research thoroughly and to present their findings in a thoughtful newspaper column.

**Make it harder!**

More able students should find out why many young people were attracted to the Hitler Youth movement, while only a few resisted. They should consider the role of propaganda and peer pressure in their analysis and write up their findings in their exercise books.

# What was the Nazis approach to young people in Germany?

## Part 1

With a partner, research education in Nazi Germany. Find out as much as you can about the way the education system was structured, what boys learned, what girls learned and how teachers were trained and treated. Once you have gathered information, write a column for an imaginary German newspaper of the mid-1930s. The column should describe what was happening to the children and young people of Germany and how this was being achieved. Write it as if you are actually living at that time, so praise the regime as you describe it.

## Part 2

This is a school timetable from Germany in 1935:

| PERIODS | Monday | Tuesday | Wednesday | Thursday | Friday | Saturday |
|---|---|---|---|---|---|---|
| 1. 8.00–8.45 | German | German | German | German | German | German |
| 2. 8.50–9.35 | Geography | History | Singing | Geography | History | Singing |
| 3. 9.40–10.25 | Race Study | Race Study | Race Study | Race Study | Party Beliefs | Party Beliefs |
| 4. 10.25–11.00 | Break – with sports and special announcements. | | | | | |
| 5. 11.00–12.05 | Domestic Science with Mathematics – every day. | | | | | |
| 6. 12.10–12.55 | The science of breeding (Eugenics) – Health Biology. | | | | | |
| 7. 2.00–6.00 | Sport – every day | | | | | |

Why do you think that German was taught so much? In Geography and History, students learned about the land that Germany used to own and how Germany used to be powerful and successful. Why was this? Why do you think that there was so much exercise and sport? Do you think that this timetable was for a girls' or boys' school and what do you think that 'Eugenics' was? Were Hitler's methods of dealing with the children and young people of Germany good?

# 44 Youth and women in Nazi Germany

**Introduction:** This lesson explores the treatment of youth and women in Nazi Germany in greater detail.

**Aims and outcomes:** At the end of the lesson, all students will understand why Hitler's regime wanted to encourage loyalty and patriotism in Germany. Most students will recognize the more sinister underlying methods and motives, and some students will be aware of German society's response at the time.

**Starter (10 minutes):** Tell students that the Hitler Youth movement had several aims:

1. To teach young people to believe Nazi ideas.
2. To prepare boys for the armed forces.
3. To make young forget about class barriers and think of themselves purely as Germans.

Ask the class whether or not they think the aims were achieved during the 1930s? They can work in pairs to research in books or on the internet to find evidence to prove that the three aims either were or were not being achieved. Then they should discuss what they have found out. Useful resources include:

*The Third Reich* by David Welch, published by Routledge, 1993

**Main phase (40 minutes):** Students are to read the task sheet and then research further resources in order to write an essay entitled 'The role of women in Nazi Germany'. They should prepare their essays by considering the ideas on the task sheet and they should write as much as possible during the lesson, finishing it for homework.

**Plenary (5 minutes):** Going round the class, encourage each student to offer one piece of evidence, one fact or one opinion about either the Hitler Youth or women in Nazi Germany.

**Suggestion for homework (5 minutes):** Essays started in the lesson should be completed.

**Make it easier!**
If some of your class struggle with essay writing, you may have to set aside some extra time in which to help them further. If necessary, show them some exemplary work that either you have previously prepared or that was completed by another student.

**Make it harder!**
More able students could work in pairs to research and compare the roles and experiences of women in the Weimar Republic and Nazi Germany.

# Youth and women in Nazi Germany

## Part 1

From the age of ten, German girls joined the Hitler Youth. By fourteen they entered the German Girls' League, where they were taught that they should aim to be a good wife and mother. A law was passed in 1933 that gave newly-weds 1000 marks – to encourage them to start a family. German women were not allowed to wear make-up or have their hair permed or dyed. They had to wear flat shoes, dirndl (gathered) skirts and no trousers. They were not allowed to diet as this was considered unhealthy for childbearing, they were not allowed to smoke and they had to wear their hair long and put it in plaits or a bun. Contraception and abortion were banned and women who had four or more children were awarded medals. Any professional women were sacked and women were not allowed to sit on any jury. Those women believed by the regime to be unsuitable were sterilized. In 1933, the first women's concentration camp was opened.

## Part 2

You are to write an essay entitled 'The role of women in Nazi Germany'. Prepare your essay by first of all considering the following:

- Why did Hitler believe that women were important?
- In what ways were women encouraged to have several children?
- What sorts of things were women discouraged to do and why?
- What were married women expected to do?
- How did the Nazis expect women to look and behave?

Once you have researched the essay and made a plan for it, begin writing it, and finish for homework.

# 45 Persecution

**Introduction:** This lesson helps students to recognize and understand what was happening in Germany – how the Nazis persecuted all sorts of people, including women who they have already studied, church leaders and Jews, but also how they seemed to bring about an economic recovery, which meant that a lot of the discrimination and intimidation was ignored or accepted.

**Aims and outcomes:** At the end of the lesson, all students will understand who the Nazis persecuted. Most students will be aware of some of the main methods they used to intimidate and victimize these groups and some students will recognize that the German people were terrified of the SS and at the same time, hopeful that the Nazis would regenerate Germany and bring many of them some hope and good fortune.

**Starter (10 minutes):** In pairs, students are to research quickly and find out what life was like for women in Nazi Germany. They should focus on what the Nazis wanted German women to do, look like and behave like. They should consider propaganda and other ways in which the Nazis made women conform and how they also rewarded women who did what they wanted.

**Main phase (35 minutes):** The task sheet tells students that they are going to research ways that Hitler persecuted German people. Ask the class to tell you what kinds of people they think might have been persecuted. See if they can come up with a list that includes:

- the work-shy
- the unhealthy
- tramps
- homosexuals
- prostitutes
- gypsies and travellers
- alcoholics
- beggars
- the mentally and physically handicapped
- juvenile delinquents
- the severely disabled
- any ethnic minorities – those who were not blond, blue-eyed Germans
- non-Christians

Put them into four groups and give each group a number from 1 to 4. They are to research for 15 minutes on their particular topic.

Group 1 – propaganda and how Hitler stirred up resentment
Group 2 – the Sterilization Law, which allowed Nazis to sterilize people with certain illnesses or perceived illnesses
Group 3 – concentration camps and, from 1936, who was being sent to them by the Nazis
Group 4 – the Euthanasia Campaign

After 15 minutes, each group is to present their findings to the rest of the class.

**Plenary (10 minutes):** Students are to draw a table of the four methods of persecution that were used by the Nazis. In the table, they should write: the names of each method, who they were aimed at, the ways they were implemented and how many (approximately) were affected.

(*continued over page 112*)

# Persecution

The Nazis believed in the superiority of the Aryan race and in order to create what they called a 'master race', they victimized anyone they believed challenged Nazi ideas, which included many minority groups. You are going to research ways that Hitler persecuted German people. What kinds of people did he persecute? Make a list.

Hitler dealt with the people he persecuted in four main ways. You are going to be in one of four groups and within your group, you are going to research Hitler's methods and present them to the rest of the class. Your teacher will tell you which group you are in, from:

Group 1 – propaganda and how Hitler stirred up resentment

Group 2 – the Sterilization Law, which allowed Nazis to sterilize people with certain illnesses or perceived illnesses

Group 3 – concentration camps and, from 1936, who was being sent to them by the Nazis

Group 4 – the Euthanasia Campaign

After 15 minutes of research, present your findings to the rest of the class.

**Suggestion for homework (5 minutes):** Students are to research why Hitler hated Jewish people. They are to write a short passage explaining this.

**Make it easier!**

If less able students are likely to sit back and not participate, have mixed ability groups, but keep an eye on them to make sure that everyone is working.

**Make it harder!**

More able students could spend an extra few minutes reading about concentration camps.

# TIPS: Persecution Topic Tips

Here are some further useful resources:

http://www.annefrank.org/
http://www.bbc.co.uk/archive/holocaust/
http://www.remember.org/educate
http://www.bbc.co.uk/history/worldwars/genocide/launch_tl_persecution_genocide.shtml

- Make sure your students understand how Hitler's early life prepared him for his ability to become a leader of Germany.
- They should understand how he changed democracy into a persecution of Jews and other minority groups.
- They should understand the terms: final solution; genocide; ghetto; Aryan.
- All students need to comprehend and then learn the facts about this topic so that they can make informed judgements. Empty opinions will be considered irrelevant by examiners. They want to see opinions that have emerged from sound knowledge and understanding of facts.
- A brief timeline of Nazi persecution against Jews:

**1933**
The Nazi party takes power in Germany. Hitler becomes chancellor. The Nazis establish the first concentration camp at Dachau.

**1934**
Hitler becomes 'Führer' or leader of Germany.

**1935**
Citizenship and other basic rights are taken away from German Jews – they cannot vote or marry Germans. The Nazis increase the persecution of various minority groups, including gypsies, Jehovah's Witnesses and homosexuals. Many are sent to concentration camps.

**1936**
The Olympic Games are held in Germany. Signs forbidding Jews from entering places are removed until the Games are over.

**1938**
On Kristallnacht, the 'Night of Broken Glass,' Jewish shops, homes and synagogues are attacked by Nazis. Across Germany and Austria 30,000 Jews are arrested. All Jewish children are expelled from schools in Germany and Austria and the Nazis take control of Jewish-owned businesses.

**1939**
Germany takes over Czechoslovakia and invades Poland. World War II begins as Britain and France declare war on Germany. Hitler orders the systematic murder of the mentally and physically disabled in Germany and Austria. Jews are required to wear armbands or yellow stars; they are not allowed wireless sets (radios) or to be out on the streets after a certain time.

**1940**
The Nazis begin extraditing German Jews to Poland; those that remain are either forced into ghettos or murdered in concentration camps.

**1941**
German Jews are not allowed on public transport and their rations are reduced.

# 46 The Holocaust

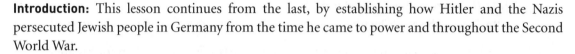

**Introduction:** This lesson continues from the last, by establishing how Hitler and the Nazis persecuted Jewish people in Germany from the time he came to power and throughout the Second World War.

**Aims and outcomes:** At the end of the lesson, all students will recognize the ways in which the Nazis persecuted the Jews, from 1933 to 1941. Most students will realize how anti-Semitism became a scapegoat for Germany's problems and some students will appreciate that others allowed the Nazis to continue their actions, whether by compliance or involvement.

**Starter (10 minutes):** Students are to complete the task in Part 1 on their task sheets.

**Main phase (40 minutes):** Go over some of the facts and dates of Hitler's persecution of the Jews and ask what students have found out about Hitler's reasons for hating them. Provide whatever resources you can and direct them to follow instructions on the task sheet.

**Plenary (5 minutes):** Ask students if they can work out what the Nazis meant when they talked about the 'Final Solution'. See if they know what the Nazis meant by the 'Jewish Question' and introduce them to the slave labour, death camps and systematic killing of Jews, gypsies, Jehovah's Witnesses and political prisoners.

**Suggestion for homework (5 minutes):** Students are to write a short essay entitled: 'How was the Holocaust possible?' This is a subject that requires students to consider a wide range of material and evidence. They should think about whom else allowed this to happen? Was it just the Nazis, or did they need the cooperation of the police, the social services and the German public? How did so many innocent people meet their deaths without somebody stopping it? How did so many people within the Nazi Party not realize the horror of what they were doing?

**Make it easier!**
This is a particularly difficult lesson, in terms of the amount of information and the topic that needs to be understood. You might find it more accessible to spread it over two lessons and to give students more guidance over the topic.

**Make it harder!**
More able students should be encouraged to read the diary of Anne Frank.

# The Holocaust

## Part 1

Create a timeline by putting each event into the correct order from 1933 to 1939.

- Kristallnacht – Nazis destroyed synagogues and Jewish homes and shops.
- From April, Jews had to register their property, making it easier for the Nazis to confiscate.
- In September, the Nuremburg Laws were passed. These were 'Laws for the Protection of German Blood and Honour'. They banned marriages between Jews and Aryans and Jews became 'subjects' rather than citizens, which meant they lost certain rights.
- In September, World War II began.
- From November, Jewish children were only allowed to attend Jewish schools.
- The Reich Office for Jewish emigration was established to promote emigration 'by every possible means'.
- There was a lull in the anti-Jewish campaign as the Olympic Games were taking place in Germany. Anti-Jewish signs were taken down.
- From June, Jewish doctors were forbidden to treat Aryans.
- In April, there was an official one-day boycott of Jewish shops, lawyers and doctors all over Germany.
- From January, all Jews had to add new first names – Sarah for women and Israel for men.
- Two days after Kristallnacht, the Nazis 'fined' the Jews one billion Reichmarks for the damage.
- From October, Jews had to have a red letter 'J' stamped on their passports.
- In September, for the first time in two years, Hitler made an outspoken attack on the Jews and more Jewish businesses were confiscated.
- Enforced segregation. Jews were banned from parks, swimming baths, restaurants and public buildings.
- From May, Jews were forbidden to join the army.
- From December, all remaining Jewish businesses were confiscated.

## Part 2

As soon as Hitler took power he worked against Jewish people, banning them from the Civil Service and other public services. Soon all Jewish shops and businesses were marked with a yellow Star of David. Read the facts and dates of Hitler's persecution of the Jews and find out about Hitler's reasons for hating them in whatever resources you can. Write an account about the following:

1. Kristallnacht – include the dates, what happened, what happened immediately after, numerical data about the destruction and why Goebbels suggested it.
2. Ghettos – research what happened to Polish Jews after 1939.
3. Mass murder – research how and why the Germans shot Jews all over Eastern Europe in and after 1941.

# 47 German economy under the Nazis

**Introduction:** This lesson helps students to recognize what life was like in Nazi Germany – the improvements and the fears – and whether the improvement of the economy was enough.

**Aims and outcomes:** At the end of the lesson, all students will recognize the changes that Hitler made to the German workforce once he and the Nazis were in power. Most students will realize Hitler's aims for the German economy and the problems he had in achieving his aims. Some students will recognize the amount that Hitler helped German workers.

**Starter (10 minutes):** Make sure that everyone reads Part 1 of their task sheets and fills in the missing words. The missing words are included on an online document, and you might like to display this after the exercise has been completed, or give it to less able students before you set the task.

**Main phase (35–40 minutes):** Using whatever resources are available to them; students should research the German economy under the Nazis. They should research and make notes about four particular areas listed on their task sheets. After making notes on those four areas, students are to decide whether or not the working class was better off under the Nazis and create a chart explaining ways that the working class was either better or worse off under the Nazis and then answer four further related questions.



**Plenary (5–10 minutes):** Discuss with the class what they perceive think was good about Hitler's economy and what was bad about it? Make sure they are aware of Hitler's promise of lower unemployment and his initiatives for industrial workers that won their loyalty. But what was the price of the benefits to workers?

**Suggestion for homework (5 minutes):** Students are to answer the question: Did most Germans benefit from Nazi rule? They are to decide who did benefit from Nazi rule and who didn't and whether the Nazi policies and activities helped most Germans or not. They should have found most of this out during the lesson, but further research will gain them more marks.

**Make it easier!**

This lesson and homework relies on students being able to conduct independent research and to write about their findings in a straightforward way. If any of your students will struggle with this, put them into a partnership with another student, and give them specific resources and places to look for information.

**Make it harder!**

More able students could work together producing their combined charts as one on the computer to be displayed.

# German economy under the Nazis

## Part 1

Read the following statements and fill in the missing words:

- When Hitler came to power, ___ million people were unemployed. He promised to deal with the problem.
- By _____, there was almost no unemployment in Germany.
- ____________ created many jobs, which meant that numbers in the armed forces increased quickly.
- Workers had no rights; they had to join the _____ _______ ______ and there were not many things to buy in the shops.

## Part 2

Using all resources available to you, research the German economy under the Nazis. Make notes on these four particular areas:

1. Small businesses (such as small shops and craftspeople)
2. Large businesses (such as department stores and large manufacturing industries)
3. Farmers (what did the Nazis think of farmers?)
4. Unskilled workers (what did the Nazis do to this group? Was it beneficial to them?)

After making notes on these four areas, decide whether or not the working class was better off under the Nazis. Draw two columns, with 'YES' on one side and 'NO' on the other. Underneath each, explain the ways in which the working class was either better off or worse off under the Nazis. Finally, answer these questions:

a. What was the DAF?

b. What was 'Strength through Joy'?

c. What was 'the people's car'?

d. What was 'Beauty of Labour'?

# Section F America

48

# What was America like in the 1920s?

**Introduction:** This lesson introduces students to the economic boom and isolationism in the US during the 1920s.

**Aims and outcomes:** At the end of the lesson, all students will understand the causes of the boom in America following World War I. Most students will be aware of ordinary Americans' fears of another war in Europe and why isolationism took place. Some students will recognize the subtler issues, including the economic problems that might have emerged from the attitudes that were being encouraged, the new industries and methods of production and the problems with the farming industry when consumer goods were selling so well.

**Starter (10 minutes):** Everyone should read Part 1 of the task sheet to introduce the topic; a good plan is to read it going around the class, so individuals read one sentence each.

**Main phase (35 minutes):** During the main part of this lesson, students are going to work in groups, finding out about the 'boom' and 'isolationism'. In small groups, of between three and five, they should research the questions in Part 2 on their task sheets. Put them in small groups beforehand and after their research, they are to work individually, writing a letter and imagining that they are American, living in the 1920s.

**Plenary (10 minutes):** Students should write down the meanings of the following words and phrases:

Republic; economic; industry; tariff; consumer goods; hire purchase; import; Congress; democratic; isolation – you could have a hands-up session for the answers just before the end of the lesson. The list of key terms is also available online for you to display on the whiteboard.

**Suggestion for homework (5 minutes):** Students are to finish writing the letters they began in class. Each should be between 500 and 600 words in length.

**Make it easier!**

As with most history at this level, this lesson is mainly research, analysis and writing. This does not suit all students, but it should be emphasized to GCSE History students that this will be required in their coursework and exam papers, so they should aim to develop skills in these areas.

**Make it harder!**

Give more able students certain check points of topics that they must include in their letters – and make these need in-depth research.

# What was America like in the 1920s?

## Part 1

When America joined the war in 1917, because of its large population and industrial strength, it tilted the balance against the Central Powers (Germany and its allies). When the war ended, the American president, Woodrow Wilson, came up with the idea of an international body called the League of Nations. This was set up to keep peace between countries. But because many Americans believed that the sacrifices they had made during the war had been a waste of money and men, President Wilson lost the US election in 1920. People were concerned that they might be dragged into another European war and so the U.S did not accept the Treaty of Versailles or join the League of Nations or the International Court of Justice. By the 1920s, America had gone through many changes. They included: an economic boom; isolationism; racism; Prohibition and the Jazz Age.

## Part 2

For the main part of this lesson, you are going to work in a small group, finding out about the 'boom' and 'isolationism'. In your group, research the following:

1. What was the 'boom' and why did it occur in the US in the 1920s?
2. What factors led to and sustained the boom and did all Americans benefit from it? (Consider the expansion of industry, advertising, mass production, hire purchase, assembly lines, higher earnings, availability of raw materials and tariffs).
3. What is isolationism, and when and why did America practise it?

Although there are only three questions, you need to find a lot of detail, which is why you are working in a group. Delegate topics within your group and pool your findings at the end of the lesson. You have about 20 minutes to research and 5–10 minutes to discuss your findings.

## Part 3

Individually – that is, not in your group – write a letter, imagining that you are an American living in the 1920s. The letter is to an English cousin, describing the boom and isolationism as it was happening in the US.

# 49 The Roaring Twenties

**Introduction:** Continuing from the previous lesson, this lesson looks at the rise in popular entertainment, the confidence of many ordinary Americans and other aspects that occurred as a result of the economic boom. It sets the background for subsequent lessons on racism and prohibition.

**Aims and outcomes:** At the end of the lesson, all students will understand how many Americans benefited from the economic boom during the 1920s. Most students will also recognize how there was little regard for the future during this period of newly found confidence and some students will be aware that this was the birth of consumerism, with the greed and dissatisfaction that accompanied it.

**Starter (15 minutes):** Ask the class whether they have heard of the expression the 'Roaring Twenties'. If any have, ask what it means or describes? Show them some images, such as of people dancing, actors from 1920s Hollywood films, vaudeville entertainers, jazz musicians, developing towns and cities, and so on. Ask students to describe the overall 'feelings' or impressions of the time (words such as fun, lively, confident, happy, enjoyable, swing, or anything similar are what you are looking for)! How and why do students think that these things developed at that time in the US? Remind them that this was after World War I. (They should consider that America was far away from Europe; that there was an economic boom [and why]; that attitudes were changing because of mass production, higher wages and other aspects of consumerism and the mix of races living in the US – what they added to the mix of cultures and styles). Individually, students are to create a mind map, showing the features of the Roaring Twenties in America. In the centre, they should write 'Roaring Twenties' and radiating out, they are to add things that were a part of that, such as dancing, design, vaudeville/music hall, music/jazz, cinema, cities, Art Deco, consumerism and so on (they should expand on as many of these as they can). They can use colour and small diagrams – anything that expresses the Roaring Twenties in the US.

**Main phase (35 minutes):** Building on the lesson starter, students are going to work in small groups of between two and four to produce a magazine that describes the Roaring Twenties in America during the 1920s. Information about the magazine's requirements is detailed on the task sheet.

**Plenary (5 minutes):** This should be a show of work in progress. Pick on each group in turn and ask them to show one of their pages, explaining what they have done and how they developed it.

**Suggestion for homework (5 minutes):** Students are to research Isolationism and why America practised it during the 1920s. They should find out what the situation was in America immediately after World War I, what the Americans feared, why many Americans were unemployed and how isolationism helped them.

**Make it easier!**
It is probable that the main task will take longer than one lesson, but if you don't want it to spread over that much study time, arrange for students to meet during a couple of lunch breaks or after school to complete the work.

**Make it harder!**
More able students could produce their magazines using a special computer program.

# The Roaring Twenties

Building on your activities at the beginning of the lesson, you are going to work in small groups of between two and four to produce a magazine that describes the 'Roaring Twenties' in America during the 1920s. The magazine must:

- Have a front and back cover, plus a double page spread in the centre. (The cover must include an image or multiple images, the names of the contributors, the name of the magazine, date, price and any lead stories; the back cover can be an advertisement, another picture or article).
- Be written as if it was created in the US in the 1920s, celebrating the situation.
- Include advertising (use your imagination and knowledge – so perhaps advertise dancing shoes, fashions, the Ford Model T, films, hotels or any other topical things you can think of).
- Include some information, such as a review about a jazz musician or a film star.
- Include something you have researched, such as a story about the President or an ocean cruise liner and anything else you have researched.

Everything must be based on fact, so research well – it cannot be completely invented and you should make a note of where you found the information.

# 50 Immigration in the 1920s

**Introduction:** This lesson introduces students to the more sinister aspects of living in the US during the 1920s and how some social groups suffered discrimination and persecution.

**Aims and outcomes:** At the end of the lesson, all students will recognize reasons why the Americans began putting restrictions on immigration during the 1920s. Most students will be aware of the social structure of the US and of the benefits and disadvantages of welcoming many different cultures into the country. Some students will understand how difficult it was for certain races and cultures to assimilate into the US at that time.

**Starter (10 minutes):** Ask the class: why did America not join the League of Nations? Students are to explain to you what they found out about Isolationism from the previous lesson's homework. They should sit with a partner and between them, answer the following questions (these numbered points are also available online, so that they can be displayed on the board):

1. When President Wilson went to the Versailles conference in 1919, he was the first US president to visit Europe while in office. Why do you think this was?
2. After joining the First World War in 1917, 10,000 American soldiers died. What do you think Americans thought about being involved with European matters after that?
3. During and after World War I, there were many German immigrants living in America. What would they have thought about the Treaty of Versailles?

**Main phase (40 minutes):** Give the class some background on immigration in the States (there is a short document available online). Everyone should then read their task sheets and follow the instructions. Firstly they are to work in pairs, researching and making notes on the new laws that American Congress created to slow down immigration. After 20 minutes, have a class discussion about what has been uncovered. Make notes about findings on the board. Do students think that these laws were a positive or a negative move? Who was restricted from moving in and why were they? Who was still allowed in and why? Was this sensible of the government or not? Now ask them to read the quotations on the task sheet and decide what they think of them. Ask them to consider the pros and cons for both quotations. Next, they are to work in pairs and list how immigrants affected American society during the 1920s. Considerations are listed on the task sheets.



**Plenary (5 minutes):** Tell the class that from 1850 to 1914, 40 million people emigrated to the US. Ask why this might have occurred. Some further background information online. You might need to select people to answer, if they don't volunteer. Accept reasons such as overcrowding in their own countries, unemployment, poverty, persecution, few opportunities to progress and so on.

**Suggestion for homework (5 minutes):** Students are to write a short piece explaining why Americans began to control which immigrants they allowed in during the 1920s. In doing this, they must categorize the immigrants and explain who was allowed in and why. Also refer to the online 'homework' assignment, which offers some good starting points for students' research; you might like to print this out and give it to some or all of the class.

**Make it easier!**
For the paired tasks, ask some less able students for their results before asking the more able students to contribute and give further substance to the investigation.

**Make it harder!**
Offer some more challenging questions to your more able students.

# Immigration in the 1920s

## Part 1

**Your task**

Work with a partner to research the new laws that American Congress created in order to slow down immigration. Make notes on the *Immigration Law of 1917*, the *Emergency Quota Act of 1921* and *the Johnson– Reed Act*, (you may find this called the *United States Immigration Act* or the *National Origins Act*) of 1924. After 20 minutes, join in with a class discussion about what you have found out.

1. Do you think that these laws were a positive or a negative move?
2. Who was still allowed in the country?
3. Who was restricted from moving in and why were they?
4. Who was still allowed in and why?
5. Was this sensible of the government or not?

## Part 2

Now read the following two quotations:

1. 'Everywhere immigrants have enriched and strengthened the fabric of American life'. (John F. Kennedy)
2. 'Unless the stream of these people can be turned away from their country to other countries, they will soon outnumber us so that we will not be able to save our language or our government'. (Benjamin Franklin)

What do you think of these comments? Do you agree with either? In what ways did John F. Kennedy think that immigrants would 'enrich and strengthen the fabric of American life' and what does this mean? If almost all the people now living in America are immigrants or were descended from immigrants, was Benjamin Franklin incorrect? Consider the pros and cons for both quotations.

Now work in pairs and, in your exercise book, list how immigrants affected American society during the 1920s. Consider:

- What did immigrants bring to the country?
- What challenges did foreign people face in assimilating into life in America?
- Does diversity encourage cultural creativity?
- How might diversity cause problems?

# 51 Intolerance in the 1920s

**Introduction:** This lesson builds on students' understanding of the changes to immigration laws and explores how and in what specific areas intolerance increased.

**Aims and outcomes:** At the end of this lesson, all students will recognize the disturbing activities that were occurring in America during the 1920s through racism. Most students will understand the unfairness of society as it developed industrially and technologically. Some students will be aware of some of the main locations where racism occurred and of the campaign of terror that the Ku Klux Klan instigated.

**Starter (15 minutes):** Allow students access to relevant reference and text books and/or the internet. They should investigate in pairs, but individually, each student should divide a page into two columns. On one side of the column, they should list all the positive things that were spreading across the US during the 1920s, such as dancing, sport, cinema, music, radio, convenience products and women getting the vote. On the other side of the column, they should list the negative things that were happening, such as prohibition, changes in immigration laws, racism, the 'Red Scare', the Ku Klux Klan and so on.

**Main phase (35 minutes):** Everyone should start reading and working on their task sheets as quickly as possible after the lesson starter. Answers to the questions should be researched thoroughly and answers written up in their exercise books for future revision.

**Plenary (5 minutes):** Discuss the Ku Klux Klan. Explain about its revival by William Simmons and how it was not limited to black people alone, but also to Catholics, Jews, homosexuals and foreigners. Explain how farmers, black Americans, new immigrants and the unemployed did not prosper in the US at that time. Ask the class why farmers and black Americans suffered – what have they learned? Why do they think that only about half the population benefited from the boom?

**Suggestion for homework (5 minutes):** Students are to research and write a short piece on Prohibition. They should explain what it was and why it was introduced? They should consider:

- The US economy in the 1920s.
- The damage to health through alcohol.
- Drunken labourers – how did this affect the economy?
- Where was beer made and why was this bad from an American perspective?
- Family problems and divorce.

**Make it easier!**

For the main part of the lesson, you could put less able students into small groups and let them answer the questions together. Some students will have greater research skills and will be able to write in greater depth.

**Make it harder!**

More able students could expand on their lists in the lesson starter for instance; they could mention names of dances, such as the Charleston and the Lindy Hop, or products, such as cars or washing machines, and so on.

# Intolerance in the 1920s

Since the new laws on immigration had been introduced, it was no longer easy to move to America from other countries. The new system favoured WASPs from northern Europe while the poor people of southern Europe found it difficult to obtain visas to allow them into the country.

In your exercise book, answer the following questions as fully as you can:

1. In what ways might the immigration policy be viewed as a form of racism (discrimination against people because of their colour/nationality)?
2. What was the fear among American WASPs about Catholics and Jews?
3. In what parts of the US (specifically) were black people feared?
4. When and where did the Ku Klux Klan begin and who started it?
5. What was segregation and where did it occur?
6. Why did the Ku Klux Klan increase (to 5 million members) by 1925?
7. What was the Red Scare?
8. What measures were taken to 'Americanize' immigrants?
9. What was the trial of Sacco and Vanzetti about? When did it happen and what was the outcome?
10. Which people in American society did not share in the boom during the 1920s?

# 52 Prejudice in the US in the 20th century

**Introduction:** Students will consider the history of black people in America, from the seventeenth century to the 1920s.

**Aims and outcomes:** At the end of the lesson, all students will recognize that America is made up mainly of immigrants and that although this should create more tolerance, for much of the twentieth century, it led to a great deal of intolerance. Most students will understand who was encouraging and inflaming the bigotry and who was working against it. Some students will understand the social and political climate that encouraged these reactions.

**Starter (15 minutes):** Everyone should read Part 1 of the task sheet and follow the instructions, answering the four questions carefully but speedily.

**Main phase (35 minutes):** Divide the class into two halves then read Part 2 of the task sheet carefully, following instructions (Part 2 also available online for display). You will need to provide plenty of relevant material for research and make sure that the groups are working well together. After 20 minutes of research, select three or four spokespeople from each group. Tell the groups that they are to present their findings to each other. Spokespeople should give clear explanations of the Ku Klux Klan and Jim Crow laws to the rest of the class and those on each side should help their spokespeople, with prompts and answering questions at the end of each presentation.

**Plenary (5 minutes):** Ask whether the American Declaration of Independence was adhered to during the 1920s and if not, how far intolerance spread in America during that time? What do students think caused such prejudices? Going round the class, discuss the probable experiences of different people, such as:

- A woman with a child whose husband had an affair and left her
- A white man whose ancestors moved to America in 1780
- A Native American
- (More examples online)

**Suggestion for homework (5 minutes):** Students are to create a chart of three columns showing intolerance in America during the 1920s. In the left-hand column, they should write down the name of a group, ethnicity or culture, such as Native Americans, African-Americans, Jews, Catholics, Protestants and homosexuals. In the middle column, they should write how intolerance affected them and in the right-hand column, they should write down the reaction of that particular group.

**Make it easier!**

This lesson introduces a variety of teaching and learning strategies, but as with most GCSE History, the emphasis is on research and writing, so the outcomes will be different according to students' abilities. Aim to keep all students engaged and interested throughout the lesson.

**Make it harder!**

More able students could research the NAACP and write a paragraph on it. The first and best could receive a reward from you.

# Prejudice in the US in the 20th century

## Part 1

Black people had been forced from their own countries to America as slaves in the seventeenth century. Once slavery had ended in the nineteenth century, in the southern states of America, there were more black people than white. Yet even though slavery was abolished, black people's lives were not improved. White governments, afraid that black people would become too powerful, introduced laws to restrain their freedom. They could not vote, they were only allowed the most mundane jobs and black children had to go to special schools that did not have the facilities that 'white only' schools had. Answer the following questions in your exercise book. Write at least two lines for each answer:

1. Was 'the Roaring Twenties' a suitable description for that period in America? Explain your response.
2. In what part of the US was life particularly difficult for African-Americans?
3. What were the origins of jazz music and many of the new dances in the US during the 1920s?
4. Explain the terms poverty and racism.

## Part 2

Even after the American Civil War, when African-Americans were freed from slavery, life continued to be very hard for them, particularly where most lived in the Southern states. There they endured poverty, intimidation and discrimination. From about 1915 to 1930, approximately 7 million African-Americans moved to the Northern, Midwest and Western states, trying to escape racism, to find better employment in industrial cities and to get better education for their children. This is part of the American Declaration of Independence of 1776: 'We hold these truths to be evident, that all men are created equal, that they are endowed by their creator with certain inalienable rights. Among these are Life, Liberty and the Pursuit of Happiness'. Do you believe this was followed by all Americans? You will have been put into one of two groups and you will either be researching the Ku Klux Klan or Jim Crow laws. Using whatever resources you can, you have 20 minutes to find out all you can on your subject and to combine it for presentations.

If you are researching the Ku Klux Klan (KKK), find out:

- When it was formed and by whom
- When and where it was reformed
- Who it opposed (make sure they note how it was not just against black Americans, but also to Jews, Catholics, Native Americans, divorcees and homosexuals)
- What tactics were used
- How they dressed
- How many KKK members there were by 1924
- The types of people who joined
- Why many of the KKK crimes went unsolved or unpunished

If you are researching the Jim Crow laws, find out:

- What were the Jim Crow laws?
- When did they begin?
- From where was the name derived?
- What did they entail?
- Who did they affect adversely and what did those people do about them?
- For how long did the Jim Crow laws last?
- What were segregation and the *Civil Rights Act*?
- Who was Rosa Parks and what did she do?

After 20 minutes, you are going to present your findings to each other. Your teacher will select spokespeople from your group. Even if you are not one of these, you should help by giving the speakers plenty of clear information and explanations of the KKK and Jim Crow laws.

# The fight for civil rights

**Introduction:** During this lesson, students will study civil rights and segregation; how African-Americans were treated within American society from the 1920s to the 1960s and how the civil rights movement was fought.

**Aims and outcomes:** At the end of the lesson, all students will understand that while many Americans were experiencing liberation and wealth, others faced intolerance and racism. Most students will understand the Jim Crow laws, segregation and the fight for civil rights and some students will understand the deep-rooted bigotry and prejudice that was experienced by many Americans of differing backgrounds or life choices.

**Starter (15 minutes):** Instruct everyone to read and follow instructions in Part 1 on the task sheet. They should answer the questions quickly in rough. After about 10–12 minutes, discuss their answers. Try to get everyone to participate.

**Main phase (35 minutes):** As in Part 2 of the task sheet, students are to work in pairs to research and make notes on one of the following people: Emmett Till, Rosa Parks or Paul Robeson.

Next, they should research and make notes on one of the following: the Montgomery Bus Boycott or Little Rock High School.

For Part 3, with their partners, students should plan and write an imaginary interview with the person they have researched. They should consider four pertinent questions to 'ask' the person and the response of that person to those questions. If they have time in this lesson, they should also write – for an imaginary magazine or website, a summary of the Montgomery Bus Boycott or the events at Little Rock High School. You may need to continue this in the next lesson.

**Plenary (5 minutes):** Discuss with the class how changes in civil rights were forced in the mid-twentieth century in America.

**Suggestion for homework (5 minutes):** Everyone should create a mind map of the civil rights movement in America during the 1950s and 1960s. Before they leave your classroom, write a list on the board of the types of things they should include or consider, such as: discrimination in voting, education, jobs, healthcare and more; Little Rock High School; the Montgomery Bus Boycott; Rosa Parks, Emmett Till, Paul Robeson, Martin Luther King and President Kennedy; the *Civil Rights Act*; the *Voting Rights Act*; in the 1950s, 18 per cent of whites and 56 per cent of blacks were below the poverty line; in 1956 the Supreme Court ruled bus segregation illegal; in 1964 the *Civil Rights Act* banned racial discrimination and segregation; in 1967 State laws on interracial marriages were declared illegal; violent racism from the Ku Klux Klan; Malcolm X and 'Black Power'.

### Make it easier!

You might prefer to spread this over two lessons. You should probably set a test at the end of this section to make sure that everyone has understood the complexities of the civil rights movement.

### Make it harder!

Particularly able students could be rewarded for completing their work early (and well) by producing their magazine or website on the computer.

# The fight for civil rights

## Part 1

In 1863, over 400 years after first Africans had been taken as slaves, slavery was banned in the US. Even then, many white Americans did not want to accept black Americans as equals. For many years, dark-skinned Americans had fewer rights than light-skinned Americans. Recap on what you already know and answer the following in rough:

1. What were a) the Jim Crow laws and b) segregation?
2. In what areas of America was there most discrimination and why?
3. What are civil rights? Who has them? Can they be taken away and if so, under what circumstances? Do rights mean responsibilities? If so, what are they? Is there a difference between civil rights and civil liberties?
4. Why did the Ku Klux Klan become so powerful in the mid-1920s?

## Part 2

Work with a partner to research and make notes on one of the following people: Emmett Till, Rosa Parks or Paul Robeson. You can choose between you which one, but choose quickly! Next, research and make notes on one of the following: the Montgomery Bus Boycott or Little Rock High School. Again, your choice, but be quick!

## Part 3

With your partner, plan and write an imaginary interview with the person you have researched. Consider four pertinent questions to 'ask' the person and the response of that person to those questions. If you have time in this lesson, also write – for an imaginary magazine or website – a summary of the Montgomery Bus Boycott or the events at Little Rock High School.

# 54 Martin Luther King and Malcolm X

**Introduction:** This lesson will help students to gain a greater awareness of the civil rights movement and its chief instigators.

**Aims and outcomes:** At the end of the lesson, all students will be familiar with the methods of Martin Luther King and Malcolm X and will recognize the importance of Martin Luther King. Most students will recognize the diversity of the people and opinions involved in the civil rights movement and some students will be aware of the context of the problems in America at that time, in relation to the social and political background.

**Starter (10 minutes):** If possible, show an excerpt from Martin Luther King's *I have a Dream* speech.

http://www.youtube.com/watch?v=PbUtL_0vAJk

**Main phase (35 minutes):** Give an introduction to Malcolm X and Martin Luther King: you might find it helpful to refer to the online background information on them (and President Franklin D. Roosevelt). You will need to make research resources available for each student. They will also need other forms of reference, including books, websites and other relevant resources. Everyone is to research both Martin Luther King and Malcolm X and produce a chart comparing them.

**Plenary (10 minutes):** At the end of the lesson, students should read the questions provided in the 'Plenary' section online (for easy display on the whiteboard), and join in a hands-up answering/ discussion session. They are allowed to look up their answers if necessary.

**Suggestion for homework (5 minutes):** Students are to write a short essay, evaluating the two activists they have studied in this lesson and give their opinion which man's goals was more likely to obtain a better life for black Americans. Essays should briefly assess the men's strengths and weaknesses and also judge whose approach was more helpful in solving the problems that black Americans faced.



**Make it easier!**
Some students will find the amount of research more difficult than debating or working in teams or pairs. These students might need further advice on resources and areas to consider within topics. If you can gather plenty of primary sources this will help to 'set the scene'. Sources could include recordings of the activists' speeches, images and articles from contemporary newspapers and other reports.

**Make it harder!**
More able students should write a short passage explaining which man's approach was better and why.

# Martin Luther King and Malcolm X

Research both Martin Luther King and Malcolm X. Both were important figures in the human rights movement in 1960s America, but they were quite different in their demands, methods and reputations. Produce a chart comparing them.

# 55 Changes for women

**Introduction:** Focusing on the changing roles of women during the 1920s, this lesson helps students understand more about many aspects of society at that time.

**Aims and outcomes:** At the end of the lesson, all students will recognize how life changed for many American women during the 1920s. Most students will realize that this was not the case for all women and some students will understand that as a predominantly religious nation, much of these changes were considered outrageous by many people throughout America, particularly those living outside large cities.

**Starter (10 minutes):** Ask everyone to consider how life changed for American women in the 1920s. Individually, they are to list as many changes as they can that occurred for women in America at that time. Let them refer to books and websites (links available online) (e.g. http://www.eyewitnesstohistory.com/snpmech3.htm, http://www.wic.org/misc/history.htm or http://teacher.scholastic.com/activities/suffrage/history.htm) or simply use their knowledge from previous lessons such as Lessons 52 and 54 to work out changes, such as having more money, more convenient household appliances, modern fashions, new dances, firmer attitudes towards husbands who drank, and so on.

**Main phase (35 minutes):** Make sure that everyone completes their list and then reads Part 1 of the task sheet. They are to write a letter, so they will need to do some additional research and possibly structure their letters in rough before completing them in their exercise books.

**Plenary (10 minutes):** Direct students to Part 2 on their task sheets and to complete the missing words exercise. The missing words are included on an online document, and you might like to display this after the exercise has been completed, or give it to less able students before you set the task.

**Suggestion for homework (5 minutes):** Following on from the previous homework, students are to research and find out whether or not Prohibition succeeded. They should make notes, explaining what happened and why.

**Make it easier!**
Make sure that everyone is managing to find relevant information. It is often helpful to stop the class at a quiet moment, discuss what people have found out and offer any words of advice or pieces of information that might spur them on.

**Make it harder!**
More able students could write or type their letters and make them look realistic by staining the paper with tea and including 'photos' printed from relevant websites.

# Changes for women

## Part 1

How did changes in society affect women? What have you included in your list? Have you considered how Hollywood films gave women more prominence; shorter, non-corseted fashions gave them more freedom and Prohibition gave them more power? What do you think that older women might have thought of the new dances and clothes? There were twice as many divorces in 1929 as there had been in 1914. What does this indicate? Write a letter to an imaginary magazine, describing how women's lives were changing during the 1920s. The letter can be one of complaint by an older woman who is shocked by the changes; it could be a letter by a younger woman who is describing how much better life is for her generation and why; or it could be written by a man who is working out why women's lives have changed so much and what effect that has on society.

## Part 2

At the end of the lesson, read the following passage and using the words at the bottom, fill in the missing words:

During the _____, especially for middle-class and urban _____, life began changing. The ________ became quite daring; many began smoking and drinking in public. Younger women no longer went out with __________, but actually went out with men before ________, without anyone to protect them!

Many had jobs – more than at any previous time in history and their work at home became easier with ___________ equipment, including _______, vacuum cleaners and washing machines. ____ were no longer just for men and they gave women ____________. By 1920, American women were allowed to _____, making them suddenly more important to the political side of American life.

* cars * marriage * fashions * independence * 1920s * vote * women * time-saving * chaperones * fridges *

# 56 The Wall Street Crash

**Introduction:** This lesson introduces the causes of the Wall Street Crash.

**Aims and outcomes:** At the end of the lesson, all students will understand some of the causes of the Wall Street Crash. Most students will be able to clarify the short-, medium- and long-term factors that led to the Crash and some students will be able to work out the links and connections between the causes of the Crash.

**Starter (10 minutes):** Introduce the topic: you may want to use the online introduction provided. Tell students that in this lesson, they are going to investigate the causes of the Crash. They can use colour and diagrams if it helps them to explain each fact.

**Main Phase (40 minutes):** The Wall Street Crash and subsequent Depression was caused by several factors. The students will divide a page in their exercise books into quarters. In each quarter, in their own words, they will attempt to explain four of the causes of the Crash and Depression. Online you will find four main causes of the Crash: these can be given to less able students, or shown on the board when the time is up. Once they have done this, they will create a mind map, using whatever resources they can to expand on their knowledge and understanding, showing the factors that led to the Crash. They may use colour and diagrams if it helps them to explain each fact.

**Plenary (5 minutes):** Going round the class, ask each student to say which two factors they believe were the most important causes of the Wall Street Crash. Once everyone has had their say, ask some to explain and discuss their reasons.

**Suggestion for homework (5 minutes):** Students are to write an account of the Wall Street Crash and its causes. They should explain what Wall Street is, what stocks and shares are and what happened in October 1929.

**Make it easier!**
This lesson involves a variety of teaching and learning strategies, reaching many different students' needs. Some students will need more assistance and guidance than others in finding relevant sources. You might need to work out individual strategies to help these, such as lunchtime or after school support sessions.

**Make it harder!**
More able students could produce their completed mind maps on computer, using colour and images.

# The Wall Street Crash

The Wall Street Crash and subsequent Depression was caused by several factors. Divide a page in your exercise book into quarters. In each quarter, in your own words, attempt to explain four of the causes of the Crash and Depression. Once you have done this, you will create a mind map, using whatever resources you can to expand on your knowledge and understanding, showing the factors that led to the crash. You may use colour and diagrams if it helps you to explain each fact.

**Useful resources**

http://www.spartacus.schoolnet.co.uk/USAwallstreet.htm
http://www.historylearningsite.co.uk/wall_street_crash.htm

# 57 The Great Depression

**Introduction:** This lesson helps students to further their understanding of the Wall Street Crash and its consequences, in particular the Great Depression.

**Aims and outcomes:** At the end of the lesson, all students will be aware of the effects on ordinary people of the Great Depression. Most students will understand the differences between the Republican and the Democrat responses to the crisis and some students will have formed logical judgements about the two administrations that occurred during the 1930s.

**Starter (10 minutes):** Reviewing what they have previously learned, students are to answer the following questions briefly:

1. What are stocks and shares?
2. How can people earn money on the stock market?
3. What made the stock market collapse in 1929?

Ask students to volunteer their answers to the rest of the class. Make sure that they all understand and recall the causes of the Wall Street Crash.

**Main phase (35 minutes):** If possible, show the class photographs of the 1930s Depression (there are some useful links online). Carefully go through the repercussions of the Crash (available online). For Part 1, put them in small groups and ask them to discuss the images between them and then, when you say (after about 20 minutes), share their opinions with the class as a whole. Ask whether anyone believes that something could have been done to prevent the Crash and subsequent Depression? Remaining in their small groups, students are to research and answer the questions provided online.

In Part 2, once they have undertaken some research, still in their groups, they are to research more fully the two presidents – that is, Hoover and Roosevelt. They are to create a chart with two vertical columns, listing the presidents' positive and negative aspects. They should include the presidents' own parties; the actions each president took to help the economy and why they did this; what people thought of each man; mistakes they made and things they did that helped the situation.



**Plenary (10 minutes):** Show the photos of the Depression once again. Ask everyone to stand up, while you pick out individuals to point out one relevant point in each photo. As each student identifies something significant, they can sit down.

**Suggestion for homework (5 minutes):** Students are to imagine that they are living in the US during the 1930s and have become victims of the Depression. They can decide who the person is and how they are facing the troubles and then each student is to write a diary entry from the perspective of their person.

**Make it easier!**
Less able students are not relying on others in their groups to do all the work. If anyone seems to be 'coasting', stop the class and ask those students about their investigations.

**Make it harder!**
Make sure that more able students are extracting detailed information.

# The Great Depression

## Part 1

Work in small groups and discuss the images. Then, when the teacher asks you, you are going to share your opinions with the rest of the class. Could something have been done to prevent the Crash and subsequent Depression?

President Hoover had believed that America's prosperity would last indefinitely and poverty would no longer exist there. He believed in 'non-intervention' – that there was no need to take any action, as the problem would sort itself out – and he made many announcements that the Depression would not last long.

## Part 2

Now you have undertaken some research, research in more detail the facts about the two presidents – Hoover and Roosevelt. Create a chart with two vertical columns, listing the presidents' positive and negative aspects. Include the presidents' own parties, the actions each president took to help the economy and why they did this, what people thought of each man, mistakes they made and things they did that helped the situation.

# 58 The effects of the Depression

**Introduction:** This lesson focuses on the consequences of the Wall Street Crash, including who was affected and the New Deal introduced by Franklin D. Roosevelt.

**Aims and outcomes:** At the end of the lesson, all students will understand why the Crash of 1929 began and many of the negative consequences of the dropping market. Most students will be aware of the drastic effects of the Depression during the 1930s and of the efforts that were undertaken to try to restore confidence. Some students will understand the situation in American life at the time and will be aware of some attempts to prevent the Crash and to overcome the Depression.

**Starter (15 minutes):** Before the lesson, prepare small cards in red, amber and green – enough for each student. Give each student one card of each colour. Then call out statements on what they have been learning (there is a list of them online). Everyone must listen extremely carefully and concentrate. You may have to repeat pertinent words or phrases to make sure that they know exactly what they are being asked about. At the end of each statement, everyone is to hold up one card of one colour. Red means they don't understand and would like further clarification; amber means they are not sure and green means that they are clear about that particular point. (For instance, what is a shanty town, what does lack of confidence in the economy mean, why were people made redundant?) You may ask any students holding up green or amber cards to explain the statement either to the whole class in general or to someone specifically who is holding up a red card. If they are all holding up red cards, you will need to spend more than just the lesson starter on that point!

**Main phase (35 minutes):** As a starting point, give some background information on the consequences of the Depression (you may want to refer to the task sheet for this). They are to use this and their own further research to find out about the impact of the Depression. Then, using their findings, they are to show significant effects in simple diagrams with annotations. Suggested images you could show are of the 1930s dust storms – the 'Dust Bowl' period. There is a selection of them available in the online document. Students are to make lists of their facts, finding as much evidence they can, in order to create their diagrams and annotations as thoroughly as possible.

**Plenary (5 minutes):** Ask students to use their red, amber and green cards once more. Project the PowerPoint presentation onto the board and go through the slides one at a time. As you announce each statement, they should react as they did at the beginning of the lesson – holding up the red cards if they don't understand, amber cards if they are not sure or green cards if they are clear about the matter. Students should be prepared to explain each statement if they are holding up a green card.

**Suggestion for homework (5 minutes):** Give students ten of the statements you have used at various points during this lesson (you can use the online 'Statements' document). They are to write explanations for each.

**Make it easier!**
Vary the pace and depth of the learning process during the various activities of the lesson by watching students' progress and application. Be aware that some of your class might be more able during some activities, but less able during others and so you need to make sure that all the challenges are appropriate.

**Make it harder!**
More able students could create detailed images from one of their diagrams, perhaps with collage or paint, to use as display material in the classroom.

# The effects of the Depression

Use the information on this sheet and your own further research to find out about the impact of the Depression, and then draw simple diagrams with annotations to show significant effects of the Depression. Here is some starting point information:

- Farmers over-cropped, meaning that they over-used the land, leading to a severe drought, which caused harvests to fail and turned the soil into dry dust which blew away, turning parts of America into a 'Dust Bowl'.
- The stock market crashed on 'Black Thursday' (24 October 1929) and 'Black Tuesday' (29 October 1929) marked the beginning of the Depression.
- Over six days in October 1929, shares crashed by 33 per cent on the New York Stock Exchange. More than $25 billion in individual wealth was lost. Later, 3,000 banks failed, taking people's savings with them.
- In 1931, 238 people were admitted to hospital suffering from starvation.
- In 1932, one in 20 farmers were evicted, 20,000 companies went out of business and 23,000 people committed suicide.
- In 1933, 25 per cent of all Americans were unemployed.
- Not all Americans suffered in the Depression. Those working in 'new' industries, such as films, electronics and aircraft continued to receive high wages.
- People who managed to keep their jobs were better off, as prices were much lower.
- As a result of the Wall Street Crash and the Depression, 20,000 companies and 1616 banks went bankrupt; 12,000 people were made redundant every day and 12 million people became unemployed.
- Some areas of the economy flourished, for instance in construction in large cities. The Empire State Building in New York was finished in 1931 and the Golden Gate Bridge in San Francisco was started in 1932.

Make lists of these facts, finding as much evidence you can, for detailed diagrams and annotations.

# 59 Roosevelt's New Deal

**Introduction:** This lesson shows students how the Federal Government reacted to the Depression and the consequences of their actions. Depending on the size of your class and the length of each news report, this might take two lessons rather than one.

**Aims and introductions:** At the end of the lesson, all students will know why President Roosevelt was elected in 1932 and the main points of the New Deal. Most students will be aware of the promises of the New Deal and the intentions behind it and some students will understand what aspects of the New Deal were helpful and what aspects were unsuccessful.

**Starter (10 minutes):** Students should read the task sheet and put the sentences in Part 1in the correct order. The paragraph in the correct order is available for you online.

**Main phase (40 minutes):** In groups of approximately six, students are to research President Roosevelt's New Deal. As explained in Part 2 of the task sheet, they should find out what Roosevelt had promised during his election campaign and as much as they can about the New Deal, so you need plenty of relevant material for them to research. Once they have gathered relevant facts, each group is to write an imaginary TV news report that gives both the positive and negative aspects of Roosevelt's New Deal. If you have the facilities, students could use PowerPoint for this. Students should consider all the measures that Roosevelt introduced and whether they worked, what they cost and what the Republicans thought of them. If you have time this lesson, groups should present their work to the rest of the class, but if there is not enough time, continue this next lesson.

**Plenary (5 minutes):** Ask students to talk about their findings. What have they found out that they did not expect? What do they think of the New Deal? What would they have done in Roosevelt's place? Allow and interchange of ideas and interrogation between groups.

**Suggestion for homework (5 minutes):** Students are to write two or three paragraphs on why they think that Roosevelt was elected in 1932? They should consider all reasons they can, which will mean doing some research on Roosevelt and Hoover as they need to know why Hoover was not re-elected, in order to develop their answer.

**Make it easier!**
Scan the classroom the whole time they are working, to spot potential problems and give further guidance if needed. If some individuals are not working well within some groups, be prepared to move some to different groups.

**Make it harder!**
More able students could be encouraged to make more of this TV presentation and to use available facilities at lunchtimes and after school to produce a professional standard 10- or 15-minute news report.

# Roosevelt's New Deal

## Part 1

Put the following sentences in the correct order:

- ☐ He became president in March 1933 when the Depression was at its worst.
- ☐ His government (the Republicans) believed in capitalism, so they did little to alleviate problems.
- ☐ Almost everyone lost money.
- ☐ Yet the president, Herbert Hoover, felt that it was not the government's job to interfere.
- ☐ 'There must be an end to speculation with other people's money' he said, and in his first hundred days in office, he passed a series of laws to try to end the crisis.
- ☐ It was estimated that by the end of Black Tuesday in 1929, 25 million dollars worth of personal wealth had been lost.
- ☐ Seen as a saviour, Roosevelt promised a 'New Deal' for the people.
- ☐ In 1932, twelve years of Republican rule came to an end as President Franklin D. Roosevelt was elected in a landslide victory.

## Part 2

In the group you have been put in, research President Roosevelt's New Deal. Find out what Roosevelt had promised during his election campaign and as much as they can about the New Deal. Once you have gathered relevant facts, within your group, write an imaginary TV news report that gives both the positive and negative aspects of Roosevelt's New Deal. Consider all the measures that Roosevelt introduced and whether they worked, what they cost and what the Republicans thought of them. Either at the end of this lesson or at the beginning of next, within your group, you will present your work to the rest of the class.

# 60 What was the New Deal?

**Introduction:** This lesson helps students to investigate the changes that were made to the New Deal and whether or not these changes were successful.

**Aims and outcomes:** At the end of this lesson, all students will understand the intentions of the first and second New Deals and the Alphabet Agencies. Most students will understand the different goals of each of the Alphabet Agencies and some students will remember the events of the first hundred days of President Roosevelt's office.

**Starter (10 minutes):** Write the following on the board:

- Investors
- Companies
- Banks
- Ordinary workers

For each, students should list how they suffered in the Wall Street Crash. The words are also available online, and can be projected onto the board.

**Main phase (35 minutes):** Give the class an introduction on the first actions of President Roosevelt in 1933. There is a 'background information' sheet online, should you wish to use it; you may want to print it off and hand it to students, or display it. In Part 1, the task sheet explains that in pairs, students are to research the first hundred days of Roosevelt's presidency and then to write a short account of them. There is a list of Roosevelt's actions online that you can give to some students, and/or display after the time is up.

In Part 2, working individually, students are to create charts as follows:

| | **Problem** | **Action taken** | **Effective or not?** |
|---|---|---|---|
| New Deal 1 | | | |
| New Deal 2 | | | |

They should add as many problems of the Depression as they can, under the heading 'Problem', so this table will fill at least one page.

**Plenary (10 minutes):** Quickly, students are to create a poster, explaining the main points of either Roosevelt's New Deal or his first hundred days. Ask them to hold them up or individually bring them to the front of the class and explain what they have done.

**Suggestion for homework (5 minutes):** Students are to write a list of the criticisms of the New Deal – what did people who opposed it say? Were they right or did they have other reasons to criticize it? They may write in bullet-points.

**Make it easier and make it harder!**

This is a varied and challenging lesson, so you will need to move around the classroom during the main activities, making sure that everyone is managing to address the issues thoroughly. Many of these are difficult issues to understand, so make sure that everyone is sufficiently motivated too. You may need to stop the class occasionally to ask what students have found out and if there are any difficulties that need to be addressed.

# What was the New Deal?

## Part 1

With a partner, research the first hundred days of Roosevelt's presidency and then write a short account of them.

## Part 2

On your own create a chart about this as follows:

| | Problem | Action taken | Effective or not? |
|---|---|---|---|
| New Deal 1 | | | |
| New Deal 2 | | | |

Add as many problems of the Depression as you can, under the heading 'Problem', so this table will fill at least one page.

# Section G International relations (2)

# 61 The League of Nations in the 1920s

**Introduction:** This lesson considers the successes and failures of the League of Nations during the 1920s. Most students will have encountered the League of Nations in several other lessons, so in this lesson a variety of factors will be considered, and students will be able to work out for themselves whether the League was successful or not during the 1920s.

**Aims and outcomes:** At the end of the lesson, all students will understand the four aims of the League of Nations and the basics of who thought of it and how it was set up. Most students will be aware of the strengths and weaknesses of the League during the 1920s. Some students will understand why the League had little chance of keeping world peace.

**Starter (10 minutes):** Provide students with books or other resources that will inform them about the League of Nations and in groups of four, they are to answer the quiz questions on their task sheets. (They may confer with their group but not with others). There is a list of the correct answers online (you may wish to display them on the board at the end), but there will be variations on these, so use your expertise to decide if the students' answers are correct or not.

**Main phase (40 minutes):** Still in their groups of four, students should follow Part 2 on the task sheet and make two lists of the League's strengths and weaknesses. They will need to research in books and/or on the internet. Online there is a list of possible answers: this could be useful for less able students or to display after the activity.



**Plenary (5 minutes):** Ask the class to discuss the following: Did the League have any chance of keeping world peace? You should chair the discussion, but make sure that everyone is heard and that they all take notes.

**Suggestion for homework (5 minutes):** How did the League of Nations work? Students are to write a short passage of between 400 and 600 words explaining this.

**Make it easier!**

You might need to vary abilities within the groups and you might find that giving *less* support and guidance is more productive with your students. Some work better when they have to research independently or by bouncing ideas and thoughts off each other.

**Make it harder!**

More able students should find out where the League of Nations was based and why it was there and not somewhere else.

# The League of Nations in the 1920s

## Part 1

1. What were the four aims of the League of Nations?
2. Whose idea was it?
3. When was it formed?
4. When did it start?
5. How many countries joined the League at the start?
6. How often did the Council meet?
7. Who did not join and why?
8. Which city hosted the League of Nations?

## Part 2

Still in your group of four, work together and make two lists; one of the League's strengths and one of its weaknesses.

# The League of Nations in the 1930s

**Introduction:** During this lesson, students will investigate the problems that developed within the League of Nations during the 1930s and its ultimate failure.

**Aims and outcomes:** At the end of the lesson, all students will be aware of the main weaknesses and errors of the League of Nations during the 1930s. Most students will understand why the League failed to take decisive action over Manchuria and some students will comprehend how the League failed to achieve its aims through such things as the Disarmament Conference and various other promises, pacts and intentions.

**Starter (10 minutes):** Working in small groups of between four and six, students are to study cartoons about the League of Nations. You may prefer to show them one, two or three images, depending on the time you are giving to this lesson starter. You may have your own resources, or there are plenty on the internet (there are some useful links in the online document).

In their groups, students should analyse the images and make notes explaining what the cartoons are saying about the League of Nations.

**Main phase (35 minutes):** Remaining in their groups, students are to research the Japanese invasion of Manchuria in 1931–33 and the Italian invasion of Abyssinia in 1935–36, and to ascertain why the League failed to prevent these events. They should read and follow Parts 1 and 2 of the task sheet. Part 2 instructs them to write up their findings as if they are writing two short newspaper columns in 1931–33 and in 1935–36, explaining: What were the effects of the League's failures in Manchuria and Abyssinia?

**Plenary (10 minutes):** Students should answer the questions in Part 3. If you wish, they could work in pairs for this. Any questions not finished at the end of the lesson should be finished in their homework.

**Suggestion for homework (5 minutes):** Students are to list seven reasons why the League of Nations failed.

**Make it easier!**
Less able students could work in smaller groups with further guidance from you, such as helping them to find information or suggesting ideas for them to follow up.

**Make it harder!**
More able students could be provided with some further questions or asked to expand upon their answers. If you are aware that some students are working faster than others, stop the class from time to time and ask these students to share tips about research and knowledge with the others.

# The League of Nations in the 1930s

## Part 1

Remaining in your group, research the Japanese invasion of Manchuria in 1931–33 and the Italian invasion of Abyssinia in 1935–36, and discover why the League failed to prevent these events. Why was Manchuria so important to the Japanese? Why did Mussolini invade Abyssinia? What made the League of Nations ineffectual in situations such as these? Is it unfair to blame the League of Nations? Share information and write individual notes on this research.

## Part 2

On your own, write up your findings as if you are writing two short newspaper columns in 1931–33 and in 1935–36. Explain: What were the effects of the League's failures in Manchuria and Abyssinia?

## Part 3

At the end of the lesson, answer the following questions:

1. How many members did the League have in the 1930s?
2. Who were the four main members of the League?
3. What did the League not have, which made it difficult to enforce its decisions?
4. What were the eight main parts of the League's organization?
5. In which country did the League set up a refugee camp?
6. Which two countries did the League send economics experts to?
7. What did the Kellogg–Briand Pact promise in 1928?
8. Why did the Disarmament Conference of 1931 fail?

# 63 The League and international relations

**Introduction:** This lesson expands on and consolidates student knowledge and understanding about the problems with the League of Nations during the 1930s.

**Aims and outcomes:** At the end of the lesson, all students will have recalled and expanded on their knowledge of the failures and successes of the League of Nations. Most students will understand more about the functions and structure of the League and some students will be aware how the occupation of Corfu by the Italians in 1923 portended what was to come with the outbreak of World War II.

**Starter (15 minutes):** Using whatever sources and resources you have, students are to answer the questions in Part 1 on the task sheet about the League of Nations. Answers (also available online for display):

1. Three times a year, or more often in an emergency
2. Settled small disputes
3. Organized the committees
4. Italy and Greece
5. Bulgaria and Greece

After 10 minutes, ask everyone to swap their answers with another member of the class to mark the work.

**Main phase (35 minutes):** Ask students the questions you will find online, and encourage volunteers from around the room to discuss. In Part 3 of the task sheet, students are to create mind maps (useful links online, some of which require the purchase of software) showing why the League of Nations failed in the 1930s. They should try to uncover new information. There are some possible answers online, useful for less able students or to display at the end.

**Plenary (5 minutes):** Ask the class to tell you at least three things that the League of Nations was successful with and at least three things it failed to achieve.

**Suggestion for homework (5 minutes):** How did the economic depression of the 1930s affect the League of Nations adversely? Students should write a passage of about 700 words explaining this.

**Make it easier!**
In this lesson, students are expected to access prior knowledge and to think around problems. Some will be better at this than others, so vary your questioning styles.

**Make it harder!**
More able students should research individually and encouraged to research beyond the normal classroom resources.

# The League and international relations

## Part 1

Using whatever sources and resources you have, in rough, write short answers to the following questions about the League of Nations:

1. How many times a year did the League's Council meet?
2. What did the Court of International Justice do?
3. What did the Secretariat do?
4. Which two countries were involved in the Corfu dispute of 1923?
5. Which two countries were involved in the Bulgaria incident of 1925?

After 10 minutes, swap your answers with another member of the class and mark their work, then swap back.

## Part 2

Join in with class discussion to answer the following questions:

1. What were the four main aims of the League?
2. Give four reasons why the League wasn't very powerful.
3. Why did the League fail?

## Part 3

Create a mind map showing why the League of Nations failed in the 1930s.

# 64 What caused the Second World War?

**Introduction:** Considering the causes and debates about causes of World War II, this lesson helps students to substantiate the origins of the conflict.

**Aims and outcomes:** At the end of the lesson, all students will be aware of the various reasons that World War II took place. Most students will understand about some of the crucial events leading up to 1939 and some students will be able to make up their own minds about the various events and occurrences that added to the likelihood of war.

**Starter (15 minutes):** Everyone should read Part 1 of the task sheet. Once they have read the points made there, show them excerpts from *Mein Kampf* and explain when Hitler wrote it. Do they think he had war in mind at the time?

Discuss: do students think that *Mein Kampf* incited war? Ask the class to try to imagine that the war did not take place – would *Mein Kampf* still have been inflammatory?

**Main phase (35 minutes):** Working in small groups or pairs, students are to work out a timeline from 1918 to 1939, including the Treaty of Versailles, the main events in Germany and Hitler's rise to power, the Great Depression and the League of Nations. In their groups, what do they think were the most significant factors of Hitler's actions during those years? Online is a selection of aspects you might want to display to the class for them to consider.

**Plenary (5 minutes):** Ask pairs or groups to discuss their timelines chronologically. For instance, pick one pair to begin by telling the class their entries for 1918–20. Write this on the board and see who has anything further to add. Follow this with 1920–22 and so on, until you have produced a class-created timeline.

**Suggestion for homework (5 minutes):** Students are to write, in bullet-point form, three or four points that Hitler included in *Mein Kampf*. Using two felt-tip pens in two different colours (e.g. purple and green) they should write by each point whether it provoked war and give reasons (one colour), or why it might not have been inflammatory when viewed from a German perspective (another colour).

**Make it easier!**
If, however, some of your students might struggle, put them with a more able partner, or group less able students together and help them with their research.

**Make it harder!**
If your students are particularly able, you might allow them to undertake the main task of the lesson individually.

# What caused the Second World War?

## Part 1

Many historians disagree about the causes of the Second World War. This lesson is to help you to make up your own mind by introducing you to some of the events leading up to the declaration of war in 1939.

1. Hitler wanted to rule the world.
2. He had no plans, but the Treaty of Versailles was simply too harsh for any country to adhere to.

You are also being shown excerpts from *Mein Kampf*, written by Hitler. Do you think he had war in mind at the time? The following two ideas from *Mein Kampf* are worth considering:

- The Treaty of Versailles must be cancelled and land that has been taken from Germany must be returned.
- The Aryan race is a master race. This was not a new idea, but it was new in the way that Hitler thought of it, believing that this race was opposite to Semitic, which referred to Jewish and Arabic people.

Join in a class discussion: do you think that *Mein Kampf* incited war? Try to imagine that the war did not take place – would *Mein Kampf* still have been inflammatory?

## Part 2

Working with a partner or in a small group, work out a timeline from 1918 to 1939, including the Treaty of Versailles, the main events in Germany and Hitler's rise to power, the Great Depression and the League of Nations. What do you and your partner or group think were the most significant factors of Hitler's actions during those years? Also consider how ordinary German citizens might have been feeling and what the French might have felt when German troops once again occupied the Rhineland.

# 65 Hitler's actions – war-inducing or not?

**Introduction:** This lesson investigates how Hitler accomplished his aims and the subsequent Second World War.

**Aims and outcomes:** At the end of the lesson, all students will understand how Hitler's aims of going against the Treaty of Versailles was largely welcomed by the Germans and accepted by the League of Nations between 1933 and 1939. Most students will recognize how short-sighted many people outside Germany were about this and how many did not think ahead of the possibilities and likelihood of trouble. Some students will make considered judgements about which of Hitler's aims were the most inflammatory.

**Starter (10 minutes):** First of all have a recap session. Ask the class to jot down notes in response to the following questions:

1. Why did Hitler dislike the Treaty of Versailles?
2. List three of Hitler's aims and three of his problems in 1933.
3. What was Britain's policy of appeasement? Do you think this was one of the causes of World War II? Explain your answer.

**Main phase (35 minutes):** Following instructions from Part 1 of the task sheet, give students 10 minutes to research Hitler's foreign policies. They can research in groups, with partners or individually as you choose. After 10 minutes, as a class, ask everyone to help you to construct a table on the board, showing, on one side, arguments in favour of Hitler's foreign policy and on the other, arguments against Hitler's foreign policy. Students should volunteer information on this, but if you are finding it difficult to extract enough from them, go around the class, selecting people to give you facts. There is a list of Hitler's aims available in the online document, which you might want to display or give out as an extra handout. With this information, all students should be able to deduce some positive and negative points. At the end of the session, make sure that they all make a note of their findings during this lesson.

**Plenary (10 minutes):** Part 2 of the task sheet explains what students are to do. In groups of three or four, they should consider facts given and select one of those facts that they think was particularly conducive to war. Go round the class and ask each group which fact they have chosen and why.

**Suggestion for homework (5 minutes):** Students are to create a mind map, showing how the Germans gained or lost from Nazi rule. They should put Germans in the middle and leading away from this, they should write in the various policies of the Nazis and whether or not they were beneficial to ordinary Germans living in Germany.

**Make it easier!**
Less able students might work better with a partner.

**Make it harder!**
More able students could write a list of Hitler's foreign policies, marking the aspects they believe to have been very important in causing the Second World War with one colour and those aspects they believe to have been less important in causing the Second World War with another colour.

# Hitler's actions – war-inducing or not?

## Part 1

Spend 10 minutes researching Hitler's foreign policies in available books or on the internet. Next, help the teacher to construct a table on the board, showing, on one side, arguments in favour of Hitler's foreign policy and, on the other, arguments against Hitler's foreign policy. Make sure you have facts to volunteer and you participate well in this exercise. Find out what his foreign policies were and deduce some positive and negative points. Make notes on your findings.

## Part 2

There were several 'hidden' factors that most people weren't aware of at the time. In a group of three or four, consider the following and select one of the facts that you and your group think was particularly conducive to war. Be prepared to justify why you have chosen your particular fact:

- The Anglo-German Naval Agreement of 1935, where Britain approved of Germany breaking the Treaty of Versailles.
- Although Hitler said he was simply uniting Germany, he also tried to take the whole of Czechoslovakia and Poland as well.
- Hitler took advantage of the weakness of the League of Nations.
- Although Hitler signed a non-aggression pact with Poland in 1934, promised not to invade Czechoslovakia and in 1936, guaranteed the independence from Germany of Poland, he went against all of these promises.

# Section H World War II

# 66 Why did international peace collapse in 1939?

**Introduction:** By considering key events and reconsidering evidence they have already covered, this lesson will help students to examine and evaluate what led to World War II.

**Aims and outcomes:** At the end of the lesson, all students will be sure of the differences between Communism and Fascism as well as recognizing the reasons for appeasement. Most students will understand how the Nazi Party was not the only reason for war breaking out in 1939. Some students will be aware of particular events of the beginning of the war and the effect these had on the rest of the war.

**Starter (10 minutes):** Students are to find out the meanings for the following words (these are also online if you wish to display them):

- Lebensraum
- Appeasement
- Communism
- Rearmament
- Conscription
- Fascist
- Policy
- International relations



(Some of these words should be extremely familiar to them, which will hopefully give them some confidence to tackle the less familiar ones).

**Main phase (35 minutes):** As in Part 1 of the task sheet, using whatever resources are available to them, students should spend about 10 minutes researching 'appeasement' and making notes on the positive and negative aspects of it. They should find out exactly what appeasement was, when and why it took place and who it was between. There are also some useful links on the online resource that you might want to share with the students, if they have access to the internet. After about 10 minutes, everyone should be ready with his or her own considered opinions as to whether or not appeasement was a wise or foolish move. They should spend the rest of the main part of the lesson writing a passage entitled: 'Was Britain's policy of appeasement justified?'

**Plenary (10 minutes):** In Part 2 of the task sheet, some quiz questions are listed. Give the class a few minutes to answer them. Here are the answers:

1. Agree
2. Neville Chamberlain
3. Germany and the USSR
4. Poland
5. 3 September 1939
6. Denmark

**Suggestion for homework (5 minutes):** Students are to research the 'Axis powers' – who/what were they and what did they want?

(*continued over page 162*)

# Why did international peace collapse in 1939?

## Part 1

Using whatever resources you can, spend about 10 minutes researching 'appeasement' and making notes on the positive and negative aspects of it. Find out exactly what appeasement was, when and why it took place and who it was between.

Areas for consideration are the Stresa Front, rearmament, the Maginot Line, the Depression, the Nazi–Soviet Pact, communism and fascism.

After about 10 minutes, be ready with your own considered opinions as to whether or not appeasement was a wise or foolish move. Consider the situation as it was then without the benefits of hindsight. Also consider possible consequences if another path had been taken. Spend the rest of the main part of the lesson writing a passage entitled 'Was Britain's policy of appeasement justified?'

## Part 2

In the remaining few minutes of the lesson, answer this quiz:

1. Did the Nazi Party agree or disagree with Italy's Mussolini?
2. In 1938, which prime minister said 'Peace in our time'?
3. In August 1939, who agreed not to fight each other?
4. What country did Hitler promise not to invade, but did on 1 September 1939?
5. On what day did Britain and France declare war on Germany (which led to World War II)?
6. In April 1940, which country did Hitler invade?

**Make it easier!**

Depending on your students' abilities, putting them in groups or with partners for the research part of the lesson and the plenary might help them to work better and formulate valid opinions.

**Make it harder!**

More able students should write a couple of paragraphs in their exercise books, explaining what they think the international leaders should have done rather than appeasement.

# TIPS: The Collapse of International Peace Topic Tips

- For this topic, all students need to know about the main terms of the Treaty of Versailles (that the German people called the Diktat), including: The War Guilt Clause, Reparations, Disarmament and Territorial Clauses.
- They need to know the order of events, Hitler's plans and how his and others' actions all led to World War Two.
- Recognising that they do not have the benefit of hindsight, all students should consider the long-term consequences of the peace treaties of 1919–23, appeasement and the roles of individuals such as Wilson, Clemenceau and Lloyd George, the failure of the League of Nations, Hitler's foreign policy and the Nazi-Soviet Pact.
- Areas that they should be clear on are: the collapse of international order in the 1930s; the increasing militarism of Germany, Italy and Japan; Hitler's foreign policy to 1939; the Saar, remilitarisation of the Rhineland, Austria, Czechoslovakia and Poland and the Nazi-Soviet Pact.

# 67 Appeasement

**Introduction:** Students will be able to build on and consolidate their understanding and knowledge of why Britain and France followed their policy of appeasement in the 1930s. This lesson helps them to develop their understanding of whether or not Adolf Hitler caused World War II and to consider other contributing factors.

**Aims and outcomes:** At the end of the lesson, all students will be aware of the reasons behind the appeasement policy. Most students will be able to develop their own theories for the reasons behind appeasement and some will develop an understanding of how far the appeasement policy went in causing the Second World War.

**Starter (10–15 minutes):** Discuss with the class what they have learned about appeasement. They should read and follow instructions in Part 1 of the task sheet. Put them in small groups of up to four, so they can list as many reasons as they can why Britain 'appeased' Hitler in the 1930s, including both positive and negative reasons. There are some possible answers online: these can be given to less able students, or displayed when the exercise is over.

**Main phase (35–40 minutes):** Everyone should read Part 2 of the task sheet and follow the instructions. They are to write an essay: 'Why Chamberlain and Daladier appeased Hitler'. As well as all they have learned so far, they should consider the ideas listed on the sheet.

**Plenary (5 minutes):** Discuss what students have found out during the lesson. What is the general overview of the reasons behind the appeasement policy? Discuss who thinks that Chamberlain and Daladier had no other option; who thinks they should have stopped or changed their tactics and what might have happened had they not given way to Hitler – what other problems might have arisen? Discuss what other countries were doing meanwhile.

**Suggestion for homework (5 minutes):** Students are to make a chart of three columns. In it, they should list at least six of Hitler's controversial actions from 1933 to 1939, such as rearmament in 1933, invading Austria in 1938 and invading Czechoslovakia in 1939. They should write the date in the first column, the action in the second column and what Britain, France or the rest of the world did in response in the third column. (If no action was taken by the other countries, they should write that).

**Make it easier!**

As with all lessons, make sure that every student is aware of the learning objectives and vary the pace. If necessary, have an extra support session or two during a lunch break or after school for those who have difficulties with the essay planning and writing.

**Make it harder!**

More able students should be able to write a short paragraph in their exercise books, explaining why appeasement was popular with many British people.

# Appeasement

## Part 1

What have you learned about appeasement? Who is the British politician most associated with the policy of appeasement? Why do many people criticize Chamberlain for appeasing Hitler? In a small group, list as many reasons as you can why Britain 'appeased' Hitler in the 1930s, including both positive and negative reasons.

## Part 2

By the 1930s, Britain and France had abandoned the Treaty of Versailles and the League of Nations as they believed they were not the way to maintain peace. Instead, they tried the policy soon known as appeasement. The British Prime Minister Chamberlain and the French Prime Minister Daladier viewed appeasement as a practical and sensible solution. They believed that Hitler's wishes were reasonable and that he would stop when he had what he wanted. Since then, many have blamed Chamberlain and Daladier for being weak cowards, while Hitler was unscrupulous and ruthless. Some have even blamed Chamberlain and Daladier for World War II. They say that by continually giving in to Hitler, he was encouraged to push them further and further to see how far he could go.

**Your task**

Write an essay entitled: 'Why Chamberlain and Daladier appeased Hitler'. As well as all you have learned so far, consider:

- whether the two men were weak;
- whether Hitler was a bully;
- when and why the policy of appeasement ended;
- what other countries were doing while the French and British were allowing Hitler to have his way;
- Winston Churchill's speeches continually warned people about Hitler and of the need to stand up to him.

When planning the essay, consider each point carefully; find evidence to support the point you are making and then explain why these points persuaded Daladier and Chamberlain to appease Hitler. Conclude with a summary of your own opinion and overview taken from all the points you have made in the essay.

# 68 Countdown to war

**Introduction:** This lesson looks at the build-up to the declaration of war in 1939. Students will be able to develop what they have previously studied and be able to make links and connections with the situation and events in different parts of the world.

**Aims and outcomes:** At the end of the lesson, all students will understand the differences between communism and fascism and the unrest the regimes caused in other parts of the world. Most students will be aware of the Nazi–Soviet Pact and of the repercussions it caused. Some students will be able to work out which events had the greatest consequences in terms of the ensuing war.

**Starter (10 minutes):** Ask the class what they understand by the terms 'communism' and 'fascism'. What is the difference? In order to be clear of the differences, they should recall and discuss the Communist ideals of Lenin, Trotsky and Stalin, but they might need to look up the meaning of fascism. Everyone is to find out which countries were Fascist and which were Communist during the mid to late 1930s and make a list.

**Main phase (40 minutes):** Read Part 1 of the task sheet carefully and instruct students to follow the task:

Each student is to produce a mind map, showing all the facts that contributed to the Second World War.

Once they have completed their mind maps, or at the end of the time you have given them for this, they should read on their task sheets about the Nazi–Soviet Pact of 1939. You might like to show them some cartoons about it – there is a small selection of these in the online resource.

Ask students to analyse these images and to explain what they are communicating. Encourage everyone to look at the background as well as the figures, the words and any details on the figures and to explain as much as they can about the images. What do they show of the West's view of the Nazi–Soviet Pact?

**Plenary (5 minutes):** Ask the class: If there had been no Treaty of Versailles, would World War II have happened?

**Suggestion for homework (5 minutes):** Students are to produce a timeline showing events that led to World War II. They should begin at 1919 and include at least 15 events or factors.

**Make it easier!**

This is a fast-paced lesson with plenty of changes of activity. Some students will thrive on this, but others might find it difficult to change the skills they have been using. Be aware of this and if anyone is losing momentum, you might have to offer support sessions or to rearrange the seating plan.

**Make it harder!**

More able students could try to produce their own cartoons to show the factors leading to war.

# Countdown to war

## Part 1

Considering so many people were against it, how did World War II happen? Recall all you have learned about events and the situation in America and Europe since World War I.

- Why were America, Britain and France in particular so against Stalin and communism?
- How did the Depression affect European countries?
- The Treaty of Versailles – was it too harsh and unreasonable or was it only fair?
- The League of Nations – was it ineffectual or was it only doing what it could?
- The rise of dictators and the extremes of fascism and communism – did some people have too much power?

**Your task:** Produce a mind map, showing all the facts that contributed to the Second World War.
Once you have completed your mind map, read the following carefully:

In April 1939, Russia, Britain and France formed an alliance to defend Poland from the Germans. Stalin suggested it, but the negotiations were prolonged. So in August of that year, Russia changed sides and made a pact with Germany instead. Known as the Nazi–Soviet Pact, Stalin and Hitler agreed not to go to war with each other and to split Poland between them.

## Part 2

Analyse the images your teacher has shown you and join in with a class discussion, about what they are communicating. Look at the background as well as the figures, the words and any details on the figures, and explain as much as you can about the images. What do they show of the West's view of the Nazi–Soviet Pact?

# 69 Why did World War II happen?

**Introduction:** This lesson helps students to consolidate their understanding and knowledge of how and why war broke out in 1939.

**Aims and outcomes:** At the end of the lesson, all students will have a clear and informed opinion of the causes of the Second World War. Most students will understand the differences between the short- and long-term causes of the war and some students will be able to make fairly complex links and connections between events and circumstances that occurred from 1919 to 1939.

**Starter (10 minutes):** Write the following on the board, or display it from the online document:

- League of Nations
- Depression
- Treaty of Versailles
- Nazi–Soviet Pact
- Appeasement
- Communism
- Fascism
- Anschluss
- Rearmament
- Reparations
- War guilt

Students are to choose any five of the above and jot down notes to explain, in a few words, why each added to reasons why war broke out in 1939. After 10 minutes, stop the class and ask individuals to explain one or two. Next, ask them whether or not each was a short-term cause of World War II or a long-term cause.

**Main phase (35–40 minutes):** Everyone should read the task sheet and consider whether or not Hitler would have been able to do what he did without the factors they have just been looking at? Ask them to help you to list issues about Hitler and the Nazi Party on the board.

Next, they are to investigate this in more depth and to write an essay called: 'Did the Treaty of Versailles cause World War II?' This will take the rest of the lesson, the following homework and possibly some of the next lesson. Suggestions of what they must include are on the task sheet. They must also include evidence to support their arguments. Offer them as many resources as possible and make sure that they consider as many causes as they can.

**Plenary (5–10 minutes):** Everyone should read Part 2 of the task sheet. Then they should consider and discuss if there had been no Treaty of Versailles, then perhaps Hitler would not have been elected. Did the Treaty of Versailles solve anything?

**Suggestion for homework (5 minutes):** Students are to continue the essay they started in class.

**Make it easier!**
Some members of the class might need some further guidance in the planning and researching of the essay. Make sure that everyone is managing to investigate as many applicable facts and gathering enough information to be able to make informed opinions.

**Make it harder!**
More able students should make references to their research and should use a minimum of three different resources per fact in their essays.

# Why did World War II happen?

## Part 1

Would Hitler have been able to do what he did without the factors you have just been considering? Help the teacher list issues about Hitler and the Nazi Party on the board.

Next, investigate this in more depth and write an essay called: 'Did the Treaty of Versailles cause World War II?' In planning, consider how much the treaty's demands initiated the war; the reasons for and effects of Hitler's foreign policy, the failures of the League of Nations, the consequences of appeasement and any of the other factors they have been considering. Make links and connections with some of the events and issues that occurred and analyse evidence to support your arguments.

## Part 2

On 30 September, Chamberlain returned to England and waved his famous piece of paper, announcing to the cheering crowd: 'I believe it is peace for our time'. The following day, the German army marched into the Sudetenland. Hitler said that it was the start of a 1000-year German Reich (empire).

**Your task:** Think about this carefully and be prepared to discuss: If there had been no Treaty of Versailles, then perhaps Hitler would not have been elected. Did the Treaty of Versailles solve anything?

# 70 The outbreak of World War II

**Introduction:** This lesson introduces some of the events at the start of the war, including 'blitzkrieg' and the 'Phoney War'. It gives students the chance to understand civilians' feelings and attitudes, experiences and propaganda and how Europe prepared for another war, 20 years after World War I.

**Aims and outcomes:** At the end of the lesson, all students will understand the feelings, fears and expectations of many Western European civilians from 1938 to the beginning of 1940. Most students will be aware of the preparations for a possible invasion and how Britain and France were not as prepared as they might have been. Some students will identify methods undertaken to protect citizens from an unknown foe. These students will be able to distinguish between the policies of Chamberlain's government and the way this was all to change with the ensuing government.

**Starter (10 minutes):** Give all students a map of Europe and ask them to write dates on the countries that the German army invaded between 1938 and 1939.

**Main phase (35 minutes):** Ask everyone to read the task sheet and follow the instructions in Part 1. They have 5 minutes to find out what 'blitzkrieg' was. Then have a quick hands-up session to work out a clear explanation.

In Part 2, everyone is to research the Phoney War – what it was like, what happened, what preparations were made and also what propaganda was produced. They are to write an eyewitness account – as a child or an adult in 1939 – and it has to describe what happened and how people felt. Some facts and eyewitness accounts are included online: it would be useful to print these and hand them out to the class. You should also provide them with further relevant resources.



**Plenary (10 minutes):** Discuss with the class: what were British people's attitudes during the Phoney War? Why did the government evacuate children? Why did parents agree to send their children away? Why did people living in the country take children in? Make sure that students make notes during the discussion.

**Suggestion for homework (5 minutes):** Students are to write a short account entitled: 'How were people's lives changed during the Phoney War?'

**Make it easier!**
Make sure that those who struggle with research and note-taking are writing down the most significant factors during the early and main part of the lesson.

**Make it harder!**
Ask more able students for more complex details in order to make sure that all are stretching themselves and gaining enough information and insight.

# The outbreak of World War II

## Part 1

'Blitzkrieg' means 'lightning war'. Now you have to do some lightning research! Within 5 minutes, find out what blitzkrieg was. Put your hand up as soon as you can give the rest of the class a clear explanation.

## Part 2

By the end of September 1939, Germany and Russia had defeated Poland using blitzkrieg. After this, Western European governments expected similar attacks on their countries. From September 1939 to April 1940, preparations for war in these countries were considerable. This period later became as the 'Phoney War' by the British, the drôle de guerre (funny war) by the French, and in Germany it was called Sitzkrieg (armchair war), because nothing seemed to happen as anticipated.

**Your task:** Research the Phoney War – what it was like, what happened, what preparations were made and also what propaganda was produced. You are to write an eyewitness account – you can be a child or an adult in 1939 – and it has to describe what happened and how people felt.

# 71 Hitler's early invasions, Churchill and Dunkirk

**Introduction:** This lesson will help students to understand and analyse what happened to the British Expeditionary Force (BEF) at Dunkirk.

**Aims and outcomes:** At the end of the lesson, all students will understand the events and significance of the evacuation of Dunkirk, most students will understand the tactics and results of blitzkrieg, and some students will be able to evaluate the events of April and May 1940 and the tactics and policies of Winston Churchill.

**Starter (10 minutes):** Write the following words on the board and ask students to write down definitions for each:

- Allies
- Blitzkrieg
- Phoney War
- Evacuation
- BEF

**Main phase (35 minutes):** Introduce the subject to the class: for this you can use the 'background information' sheet available online. In Part 1 of the task sheet they are instructed to write a newspaper article based on the events of Dunkirk, imagining that they are in Europe during May and June 1940. They will need to research events, opinions and evidence in order to formulate an attention-grabbing and thorough article.



**Plenary (10 minutes):** If possible, play some of Churchill's speeches to the class. Then they are to read two of his speeches for Part 2 of the task sheet. These are available online and should be printed off and handed out to the students. Everyone is to consider the impact of Churchill's speeches to the British people. Did they make the people more determined to fight the Germans or not? In what ways would it have roused people? Ask for intelligent comments about emotion, tenacity, fortitude and the methods he used to inspire.

**Suggestion for homework (5 minutes):** Students are to research and write a short analysis of selected speeches delivered by Winston Churchill during World War II. Remembering comments in the plenary, they should write how the speeches strengthened the British resolve to fight the Germans.

**Make it easier!**

Less able students may require extra time to write their articles, so you might need to arrange support sessions outside the usual lesson, or to allow them to continue during the next lesson.

**Make it harder!**

Encourage more able students to find less-well-known examples of Churchill's speeches.

# Hitler's early invasions, Churchill and Dunkirk

## Part 1

Your task: Write a newspaper article based on the events of Dunkirk, imagining that you are in Europe during May and June 1940. You will need to research events, opinions and evidence in order to formulate an attention-grabbing and thorough article. How did the events at Dunkirk make the British feel about the war?

## Part 2

Consider the impact of Churchill's speeches to the British people. Did they make the people more determined to fight the Germans or not? In what ways would it have roused people? It's the end of the lesson, but you should still be thinking deeply about emotion, tenacity, fortitude and the methods he used to inspire.

# The Battle of Britain and the Blitz

**Introduction:** Continuing with events in World War II, this lesson shows how the Battle of Britain changed the direction of the war and how the Blitz affected civilians.

**Aims and outcomes:** At the end of this lesson, all students will be aware of the repercussions of the Battle of Britain and the effects of the Blitz. Most students will understand the consequences of the war, including the occupation of France, the Battle of the Atlantic, the Battle of Britain and the Blitz. Some students will be familiar with the events, attitudes and procedures for coping with the bomb attacks.

**Starter (10 minutes):** Working with a partner, students have 10 minutes to research: What was the Battle of Britain? When the 10 minutes is up, go round the class asking each pair to give a fact each about the Battle of Britain. Write salient points on the board. These could include the occupation of France and the Battle of the Atlantic as well as the Luftwaffe and its objectives in overcoming the Royal Air Force.

**Main phase (35 minutes):** You should display the online resource about Operation Sea Lion to the class. In Part 1 of the task sheet, they are to work in pairs, finding out and listing in detail as many facts as they can find about the Blitz. There is a list of possible facts online, to be handed out to less able students or to be displayed when the exercise is over.

**Useful resources**
*The Times London History Atlas*, edited by Hugh Clout, Times Books, 1997
*London: The Biography*, Peter Ackroyd, Vintage, 2001
Plus useful links online

In Part 2 of the task sheet, they are to find out information about other types of bombs that targeted London.

**Plenary (10 minutes):** Tell everyone that they have 10 minutes to write down five ways in which the government tried to protect people from the Blitz.

**Suggestion for homework (5 minutes):** Students should divide a page into two columns. Under the heading 'Was the Battle of Britain a turning point in World War II?' they should list reasons why it was on one side and why it wasn't on the other side.

**Make it easier!**
Mixed ability pairs can be helpful for some less able students.

**Make it harder!**
More able students could write their findings as a poster, using the computer or collage materials to make it eye-catching.

# The Battle of Britain and the Blitz

## Part 1

**Your task:** Working with a partner, find and list, in detail, as many facts as you can find about the Blitz.

## Part 2

Find out information about other types of bombs that were used on London:

The Germans continued to bomb Britain throughout the war. From 1944, they used two new weapons known as flying bombs. The V1 (Doodlebug/Buzz bomb/Flying bomb) came first, recognized by the sound of the buzzing engine. As soon as the noise stopped, the bomb fell to earth and everyone had only 15 seconds to run. Almost 9,250 V1s fell in London, but less than 2,500 reached their targets. About 2,000 were destroyed by anti-aircraft gunfire, 2,000 by fighter planes and almost 300 by barrage balloons. The V2 were long-distance rockets that arrived without any warning sound. They flew fast and far too high to be shot down by anti-aircraft guns. They were so powerful that they could flatten whole streets.

# 73 What happened on D-Day?

**Introduction:** This lesson focuses on the D-Day landings.

**Aims and outcomes:** At the end of the lesson, all students will understand many of the events and tactics employed by the Allies during the D-Day landings. Most students will be aware of the reasons that the Allies eventually won the war and some students will be aware of the consequential weaknesses of Britain after the war.

**Starter (10 minutes):** Explain to the class that in 1941, Hitler proceeded with plans to defeat the Soviet Union and, at the end of that year, he also declared war on the US, but it still took another three years for the Allies to defeat Germany. Using as many sources and resources as they can, students are to work in small groups, plotting a timeline of the war, from September 1939 to May 1945. Each group should include at least 20 significant dates in their timelines.

**Main phase (35 minutes):** Provide everyone with a map of southern Britain, the English Channel and northern France. After your explanations, ask them to research and plot where the Normandy Landings took place. They should read Parts 1 and 2 of their task sheets and, in the small groups from the lesson starter, they are to research the D-Day Landings and produce an A3 or A2 poster, showing how the Allies achieved their aim. There is a brief description online of the D-Day events that you may wish to read out or display to the class.

**Useful resources**

http://www.britannica.com/dday
http://news.bbc.co.uk/onthisday/hi/dates/stories/june/6/newsid_3499000/3499352.stm

**Plenary (10 minutes):** Ask everyone to write down three questions about the D-Day Landings. Next, choose one person to ask another person one of his or her questions. If that person can't answer it, then anyone who can answer it should put up a hand and volunteer the answer. Whoever has answered correctly can then pose one of his or her questions to a person of their choice in the class. Make sure that everyone gets a chance to answer a question and that the questions are answered coherently and correctly.

**Suggestion for homework (5 minutes):** What were the effects of the war on Britain? Students are to think about the ways in which Britain was damaged at the end of the war. They should consider, not only the physical damage caused by bombs, but also the financial trouble, the lack of progress made in industry and the trade that had been lost during that time. They should make thorough notes, adding specific details, such as information about jobs, money owed to America and the costs of rebuilding and economic recovery.

**Make it easier!**
Mixed-ability pairs can be helpful for some less able students.

**Make it harder!**
More able students could write their findings as a poster, using the computer or collage materials to make it eye-catching.

# What happened on D-Day?

## Part 1

You should have a map of southern Britain, the English Channel and northern France. You are going to research and plot where the Normandy Landings took place.

## Part 2

In the small group you were in at the start of the lesson, you are to research the D-Day Landings and to produce a poster on A3 or A2 paper, showing how the Allies used bravery, clever tactics and new technologies to achieve their aim.

# 74 How were women affected by the war?

**Introduction:** This lesson helps students to consider the role of women in the Second World War, including the work they did, how rationing, jobs and conscription affected them, the Women's Land Army and evacuation.

**Aims and outcomes:** At the end of the lesson, all students will understand why women's roles in the war effort were essential. Most students will be aware of the reasons that the strength of everyone during the war added to the ultimate outcome and some students will recognize the wider repercussions that occurred after the war and the changes to society this engendered.

**Starter (10 minutes):** There is a quick multiple-choice quiz for this part of the lesson in Part 1 of the task sheet.

**Main phase (35 minutes):** As in Part 2 of the task sheet, students are going to find out about the role of women in Britain during World War II. They should investigate the points listed on the task sheet and make detailed notes on their findings.

**Plenary (10 minutes):** In pairs, students are to present back to the rest of the class, the different ways in which women contributed to the war effort during World War II.

**Suggestion for homework (5 minutes):** Students are to find out and answer the questions in Part 3 of their task sheets.

**Make it easier!**
Only give extra support and guidance to those students who seem to need it – some do better by working independently – but keep checking that everyone is remaining focused throughout the various activities of the lesson.

**Make it harder!**
More able students could produce mind maps as well for extra explanation.

# How were women affected by the war?

## Part 1

You have 10 minutes to do this multiple-choice quiz:

1. Before World War II, married women were expected to:
   a. run businesses
   b. be housewives
   c. join the armed forces
2. Conscription for single women began in:
   a. 1941
   b. 1943
   c. 1939
3. The organization for women conscripted to work on farms was called:
   a. the Women's Land Army (WLA)
   b. the Women's Voluntary Service (WVS)
   c. Women Working on Farms (WWF)
4. When women worked during the war, they were paid:
   a. the same as men
   b. more than men
   c. a lot less than men

## Part 2

You are going to find out about the role of women in Britain during World War II. Investigate the following points:

- What difference did the war make to married women's lives?
- What jobs did women undertake during the war?
- Considering that women were usually the homemakers, how did rationing affect them?
- How did wartime propaganda target women?
- What did women do in the military forces?
- How did women's contribution affect the war effort?
- Collect information on the Air Transport Auxiliary (ATA), Women's Land Army (WLA) and Factory Work, Women's Voluntary Service (WVS) and the Auxiliary Territorial Service (ATS).

Make detailed notes on your findings.

## Part 3

1. Why was rationing introduced?
2. When was rationing introduced?
3. What was rationed?
4. How did rationing work?
5. What were ration books?
6. Was rationing fair?

# The effects of the Second World War

**Introduction:** This lesson – which you might prefer to spread over two – enables students to attain greater understanding of the impact and effects of World War II.

**Aims and outcomes:** At the end of the lesson, all students will understand the general impact of the war internationally, politically and locally. Most students will be aware of how the war changed the world, politically and socially and some students will appreciate the wider connotations of the UN, the World Bank, the European Union, the Marshall Plan and the rise of the superpowers.

**Starter (10 minutes):** Explain to the class that you are going to consider the impact of the war. Under the following headings, working in small groups, students are to list all the ways in which the war affected them (also online for easy display):

- Civilians across the globe
- Politics
- Life in Britain

This is also in Part 1 of the task sheet.

**Main phase (35 minutes):** Have a quick round-up of what everyone has found. Discuss and list essentials on the board. As in Part 2 of the task sheet, they are now going to research this in greater depth, but within each group they are going to choose one of the three areas to research, and then present their findings to the rest of the class. Some facts are listed online; you might find it useful to print these and hand them out to students to help each group to choose which area they will research.

They are going to present their findings to the rest of the class. For this lesson, they should research and make notes on all of the effects of the war that they can find relating to their heading. They should try to find evidence and sources to underpin their findings.

**Plenary (10 minutes):** The effects of World War II had huge repercussions on the international community. As a class, discuss and list as many negative and as many positive effects as you can. List them in two columns on the board and with students writing the lists in their books at the same time.

**Suggestion for homework (5 minutes):** If you are continuing this lesson into a further lesson, allow students this homework time to collect more material and information for their presentations, to be given next lesson. If you have managed to do this all in one lesson (if you have a particularly small group) then ask them to write a short interview with someone from the war – their choice entirely. Suggestions could be an ex-prisoner of war, a survivor of the Holocaust, a wife and mother from Coventry, a soldier, or a London child. This interview is for a short radio broadcast. What ten questions will the interviewer ask and what ten answers will the interviewee respond with?

**Make it easier!**

As in previous lessons, mixing abilities can be helpful in some classes. If this will not be effective with your class, try seating groups where you can keep a close eye on certain students.

**Make it harder!**

Allow more able or diligent groups access to further resources.

# The effects of the Second World War

## Part 1

Consider the impact of the war. Working in a small group, under the following headings, list all the ways in which the war affected them:

- Civilians across the globe
- Politics
- Life in Britain

## Part 2

In the class discussion, volunteer information that you have found out. Then in the small group you were just in, research just one of those headings in greater depth. Choose the heading you will research – you will be presenting your findings to the rest of the class later in the lesson.

For this lesson, research and make notes on all of the effects of the war that you can find relating to your heading. Discuss what you will tell the rest of the class – images will help too. Try to find evidence and sources to underpin your findings.

## Part 3

The effects of World War II had huge repercussions on the international community. Join in a class discussion and help to create a list of as many negative and as many positive effects as you can. As the teacher lists them on the board, create the list in your exercise book, in two columns.

**Final thoughts:** Millions of lives had been lost and Germany was divided into four occupation zones, controlled by the United States, Great Britain, France and the Soviet Union. Many European borders were redrawn and Israel was created, the welfare state developed in Britain, and communism spread to China and Eastern Europe. Many organizations emerged including, in an effort to maintain international peace, the United Nations. Technologies, such as computers and jet engines, also appeared during this period. After World War II, the world was dominated by two powerful countries – the United States and Soviet Union – which became known as the superpowers.

# Section I The Cold War

# 76 The beginnings of the Cold War

**Introduction:** This lesson investigates the rise of the superpowers and the beginnings of the Cold War.

**Aims and outcomes:** At the end of this lesson, all students will be aware of the agenda at Yalta in 1945 and the relationship between the 'Big Three' at the start of the meeting. Most students will appreciate the reasons their views differed and some students will recognize the reasons why Churchill and Roosevelt became suspicious of Stalin.

**Starter (10 minutes):** Introduce capitalism and communism and help students to list the main features of each in two columns. For instance:

| Capitalism | Communism |
|---|---|
| Opportunity for everyone<br>Free economy<br>Private enterprise | Equality for all<br>Common ownership<br>Classless society |

The table is also available online for easy display.

**Main phase (40 minutes):** Everyone should read Part 1 of the task sheet carefully. Make sure that everyone in the class understands. After they have had time to read and consider, ask students individually and around the class if they understand specifics. Once you have made sure that everyone is clear about the situation in 1945, ask them to read Part 2 about what happened at Yalta in February 1945. Students may work in pairs to research what occurred at Yalta. They are to find reliable sources and investigate the meeting. With their partners, they are to list each of the items on the agenda and to write down a) whether the three representatives agreed or not and b) what was decided.

**Plenary (5 minutes):** As far as anyone outside the meeting was concerned, the three were united against Hitler, but within the conference, was everything going so smoothly? Discuss over what and why the Big Three did not agree. How and why did the alliance break down?

**Suggestion for homework (5 minutes):** Students should answer the questions in Part 2 of the task sheet.

**Make it easier!**
Mixed ability pairs might be helpful in providing support for less able students. Some less able students might need more structure and guidance in finding valid information and sources.

**Make it harder!**
More able students could write a short article on the beginnings of the Cold War, imagining they are newspaper reporters in about 1946.

# The beginnings of the Cold War

## Part 1

Read the following facts carefully:

- The USSR lost around 20 million people in World War II, Great Britain lost around 370,000 and America lost about 297,000.
- Before World War II several countries could have claimed to be superpowers. These were: the US, USSR, Great Britain, France, Japan and Germany.
- The damage caused by the war to these countries left only two countries with the military strength and resources to be called superpowers. These were the US and USSR.
- US was capitalist and USSR was communist.

Make sure you understand the situation in 1945, and if not, ask or research it further. It is important that you are clear. Then read this:

The Yalta Conference is often cited as the beginning of the Cold War. It was a meeting of the 'Big Three' at the former palace of Tsar Nicholas on the Crimean southern shore of the Black Sea. It took place from 4 to 11 February 1945 and it was to decide the fate of post-war Europe. The United States was represented by Franklin D. Roosevelt, Great Britain was represented by Winston Churchill, and Josef Stalin represented the Soviet Union. On the agenda was:

- The dividing up of Germany
- The formation of the United Nations
- German war reparations
- The entry of Soviet forces into the Far-Eastern front (Japan)
- The future of Poland

You may work with a partner to research what occurred at Yalta. Find reliable sources and investigate the meeting. With your partner or on your own, list each of the items on the agenda and write down:

a. whether the three representatives agreed or not and

b. what was decided.

## Part 2

1. What was the main objective of the Yalta Conference in 1945?
2. What was agreed about the formation of the UN?
3. Why did Roosevelt and Churchill disagree with Stalin over the future of Poland?

77

# The Cold War

**Introduction:** This lesson helps students to recognize some of the causes behind the Cold War and events during it. They will be able to see clearly how relationships between the two superpowers broke down after World War II and why.

**Aims and outcomes:** At the end of the lesson, all students will recognize some of the causes behind the Cold War. Most students will understand the ways in which the two superpowers worried each other and made the situation worse, such as the Marshall Plan, the Truman Doctrine and the Berlin Blockade. Some students will appreciate the consequences of all of these.

**Starter (10 minutes):** Show the class some paintings by Norman Rockwell, painted in 1943 (there is a good selection of links to these in the online resource). Tell the class about Norman Rockwell using the brief online biography provided. Ask students to note when they were painted and to try to analyse what each painting is saying. What does this say about the American people – at the time and in general? What do students think that the rest of the world might have thought of the sentiments? For instance, would Stalin have agreed with any of them?

**Main phase (35 minutes):** Ask students if they know what is meant by the following:

- Marshall Aid
- Truman Doctrine
- Iron Curtain
- Democracy
- Containment
- Domino Theory
- Cold War

Encourage them to have a go, even if they get it wrong. Next, they should read the task sheet and, within their groups, find out and answer the questions listed.

**Plenary (10 minutes):** Still within the groups – or try putting two groups together – students are to produce a timeline showing the events of the Cold War, from 1945 to the building of the Berlin Wall in 1961.

**Suggestion for homework (5 minutes):** What were the nuclear arms race and the Cuban missile crisis? Students are to research these issues and make notes to present to the class in the next lesson.

**Make it easier!**

Go around the class if possible, armed with ideas and suggestions for resources and distribute appropriate tasks within groups, without making it obvious that some are more difficult than others. (No one ever said that differentiation is easy!)

**Make it harder!**

More able students could try one of the online quizzes, such as:

http://www.schoolhistory.co.uk/lessons/coldwar/change_matchup.html
http://www.schoolhistory.co.uk/lessons/coldwar/truman_matchup.html

# The Cold War

After Yalta, the next meeting of the 'Big Three' was in Potsdam in July to August 1945. By then, two of the people had changed – Truman, who was more anti-Communist than Roosevelt, had taken over as US President, and Churchill had lost the general election, to be replaced by Prime Minister Attlee in Britain. At Potsdam, few issues were agreed and several issues were left with no final decision. After Potsdam, the US and the USSR were very suspicious of each other.

Within your group, find out and write answers to the following questions in your exercise book:

1. What was the Marshall Plan and why was it introduced?
2. Who – if anyone – was to blame for the Cold War?
3. Why was Soviet espionage such an important issue?
4. What impact did Joseph McCarthy have on American anti-communism?
5. Why did the USSR boycott the UN in 1950 and what did this allow Truman to do?

# 78 The collapse of communism

**Introduction:** By this lesson, students should have studied the arms race, the Korean War, the Berlin Wall and the Berlin airlift, the Cuban missile crisis, the Vietnam War and the Suez Crisis. This lesson will help them to further their understanding of détente and the collapse of communism.

**Aims and outcomes:** At the end of the lesson, all students will understand why communism began collapsing in the 1980s. Most students will recognize many of the factors that contributed to this, including the rise of nationalist resistance to the ideology of communism that had started in the 1950s and changes in the international political environment. Some students will understand that the failure of the Soviet leadership to devise suitable reforms and the arms race also contributed to the breakdown.

**Starter (10–15 minutes):** In Part 1 of the task sheet, there is short quiz for students to work on in small groups of four. Compare answers after 10 minutes.

**Main phase (35–40 minutes):** Everyone needs to understand the events of the 1950s, 60s and 70s. In Part 2 of the task sheet, there are suggested websites for them to find out more about détente and the collapse of communism. In Part 3, they are asked to find out further information, so provide relevant resources as they are then going to produce the front page of a newspaper, announcing the end of communism. If necessary, this could take another lesson.

**Plenary (5 minutes):** Compare the work that everyone has completed.

**Suggestion for homework (5 minutes):** Students should reply to the following statement: 'Gorbachev was responsible for the collapse of the USSR. Discuss'.

**Make it easier!**
Less able students might need to take at least two lessons for this particular topic with a recap test at the end.

**Make it harder!**
More able students could produce their front page on the computer, making it look as professional as possible.

# The collapse of communism

## Part 1

In 10 minutes, answer the following short quiz:

1. In what year was the Berlin Wall built?
2. Who was overthrown by Fidel Castro in 1959?
3. Which treaty was signed as a consequence of the Cuban missile crisis?
4. Which South Vietnamese ruler was overthrown in 1963?
5. What did America do to prevent Soviet missiles reaching Cuba?
6. In what year was Vietnam joined under communist rule?

## Part 2

To understand the events of the 1950s, 60s and 70s, research one or two of the following sites to find out about détente and the collapse of communism:

**Useful resources**

http://www.historylearningsite.co.uk/detente.htm
http://www.bbc.co.uk/schools/gcsebitesize/history/mwh/ir2/endofthecoldwarrev1.shtml

## Part 3

In your group, find out the following:

- Why was the USSR in crisis in the 1980s?
- What were Glasnost and Perestroika?
- How did Gorbachev help to end the Cold War?
- When and why was Boris Yeltsin elected President of Russia?

You are to produce the front page of a newspaper, announcing the end of communism. Think of a thought-provoking or attention-grabbing headline and carefully select an image or two. Write your words in short and long sentences, making sure that every sentence contains a fact.

# Recommended resources

In addition to resources mentioned in specific lessons, the following books and websites could be useful.

## Books for students

*World War I*, H. P. Willmott (London: Dorling Kindersley, 2008)
*GCSE History: Student Workbook: Modern World History, 1900–49*, Geoff Layton and Nick Dyer (London: Philip Allen, 2006)
*London: The Biography*, Peter Ackroyd, (London: Vintage, 2001)
*The Limits of Liberty: American History 1607–1992*, Maldwyn A. Jones, (Oxford: OUP, 1995)
*We Shall Overcome: The History of the American Civil Rights Movement (People's History)*, Reggie Finlayson (Minneapolis: Lerner Publishing Group, 2002)
*The Russian Revolution and the Soviet Union 1910–1991 (GCSE Modern World History for Edexcel)*, John Wright and Steven Waugh (London: Hodder Murray, 2006)
*The Russian Revolution (Days That Shook the World)*, Paul Dowswell (London: Wayland, 2003)
*Women's War (At Home in World War II)*, Stewart Ross (London: Evans Brothers, 2007)
*Rationing (At Home in World War II)*, Stewart Ross (London: Evans Brothers, 2007)
*World War II (I Can Remember)*, Sally Hewitt (London: Franklin Watts, 2003)
*The Causes of World War II (Questioning History)*, Stewart Ross (London: Wayland, 2003)
*The Cold War 1945–1991 (Collins Frontline History)*, Derrick Murphy (Glasgow: Collins Educational, 2003)
*Mastering Modern World History (Palgrave Master)*, Norman Lowe (Basingstoke: Palgrave Macmillan, 2005)
*Documenting History: Slavery and Civil Rights*, Philip Steele (London: Wayland, 2009)
*Documenting History: World War I*, Philip Steele (London: Wayland, 2009)
*20th Century Lives: Campaigners*, Philip Steele (London: Wayland, 2010)
*The Third Reich*, David Welch (New York: Routledge, 1993)
*The Times London History Atlas*, edited by Hugh Clout (London: Times Books, 1998)

## Books for teachers

*Essential Modern World History: Teachers' Book (History in Focus)*, Ben Walsh (London: Hodder Murray, 2003)
*GCSE Modern World History: Teacher's Resource Book (History in Focus)*, Ben Walsh (London: Hodder Murray, 2002)
*Modern World History for AQA B: Foundation Teacher's Resource Pack*, John Derrick, Tony Hewitt and Steve Waugh (Oxford: Heinemann Educational Publishers, 2001)

## Useful websites

http://www.spartacus.schoolnet.co.uk/
http://www.schoolhistory.co.uk
http://www.free-teaching-resources.co.uk/history_key_stage_4.shtml
http://www.spartacus.schoolnet.co.uk/historywebsites.htm
http://www.historylearningsite.co.uk/index.htm
http://www.teachers.tv/search/node/KS4+History
http://www.great-britain.co.uk/history/history.htm
http://www.bbc.co.uk/schools/gcsebitesize/history/
http://www.smithsoniansource.org/

**The following websites require a subscription, but are worth having**

http://www.britannica.com
http://www.bridgemaneducation.com
http://histclo.com/youth/youth/org/nat/hitler/hitlerhwy.htm